I Survived Hitler

The Story of Linda Ryngermacher Fishman

Written and compiled by
CLAUDIA HOLMES

With contributions by Carolyn Holmes
and Ann Fishman Baum

Text edited by Susan Sommer, MFA

Copyright © 2014 Claudia Holmes
All rights reserved.

ISBN: 1500279005
ISBN 13: 9781500279004

Many of the survivors will not talk about the Holocaust, even to their own children. When the survivors die out, there will be no one left to be a living witness. I speak about the Holocaust because I want the whole wide world to know about it. I want to call attention to it, and I want people to remember it. I tell people, stand up for human rights! I tell the story for the sake of my children, my grandchildren, and my great grandchildren. If this happened to me and my family, what makes you think it couldn't happen to yours? Please, don't let anything like this ever happen again.

(Compilation from interviews with Linda Fishman)

CONTENTS

Introduction ix

Acknowledgements xiii

Linda Fishman 1
Growing up

Claudia Holmes 5
Beschert
Our Friendship Grows
Visiting Linda

Linda Fishman 23
German Occupation

Carolyn Holmes 29

Linda Fishman 33
My Parents' Capture
Skarzysko

Claudia Holmes 49

Linda Fishman 53
Czestochowa
Cattle Trains

Bergen Belsen
Burgau
Turkheim
Death March
Allach
Liberation
Feldafing
Immigrating to America

Ann Fishman Baum. 85
Impact of the Holocaust; the daughter of survivors

Claudia Holmes 89
Farewell

Epilogue 97

Timeline of Events. 115

Glossary 121

For Luba and Chana

INTRODUCTION
I Survived Hitler is a story of faith, family, and perseverance.

Linda Ryngermacher Fishman survived as a living witness to the Holocaust. This story is based on her own memories. The dates and experiences as described in the manuscript have been validated to the extent possible.

Linda discussed the sub-human conditions and torture endured in the camps, but she did not disclose graphic details. The depth of her actual experience is more than what is described on the pages of this manuscript. As with most survivors, some experiences are either too horrific to remember or too emotional to talk about. I did not fill in supplemental details of the camps or experiences other than what she provided. Many sources are available from which to obtain more detail, should one choose to do so.

Toward the very end of Linda's imprisonment she may have remembered some details in a sequence other than how they occurred. She recalled seeing the sign *Albeit Macht Frei* over the gates of Bergen-Belsen. It was instead over the gate at Dachau, and she would have seen it on the Death March to Allach. Linda described sleeping on the ground at Burgau, though it was more likely the sleeping arrangements at Turkheim.

Both details were at a time when she was just barely holding on to life, and minor items would have been easily crossed in memory.

The Holocaust stole Linda's childhood and destroyed her family. Her formal education stopped at the sixth grade. From the age of fourteen, she lived in a war zone with escalating violence and an unimaginable outcome. It was through that lens that Linda viewed the rest of her life. Every experience she had from that point on related in some way to what she endured in and after the Holocaust. It affected her perception of life in America, her parenting style, and her very existence.

Linda started her life in America as a shy young woman, living in a world she did not understand. She initially felt that the community did not welcome them, and that they had been left to fend for themselves in a foreign land. In time, she grew to embrace life in Des Moines and to love the community. She was unfazed by any challenge, either personal or professional.

Linda had a vibrant personality and boundless energy. She had her own sense of personal style, choosing bright colors and patterns because they made her happy. Orange and red were a favorite color combination, and she would finish off her look with bright red lipstick. For special occasions, she would add a hat.

Linda was outspoken and bold, though some would describe it as brash and unfiltered.

"To say she had strong opinions is an understatement," said friend Shirley Berg.

Rabbi Marshall Berg added, "In Hebrew we have a saying that translates From the Lungs to the Tongue." Linda freely said what was on her lungs, and tact was not her strong suit. You never knew what she might say next, but you always knew where you stood with her.

Linda loved to be with people and she had many friends. "*Everybody* knew Linda!" said Shirley, and Barbara Geller, another friend.

Linda never missed a celebration and if dancing was involved, she was the first on the dance floor, gathering people in her wake. Holidays were

I Survived Hitler

important to her, especially the Sabbath Day, both as part of Judaism and for the memories of family celebrations when she was young.

Linda treasured her children, her grandchildren, and her great grand-children. She wanted them to know her story, and to understand what she went through. She wanted them to appreciate life, to be strong in their faith, and to never, ever, forget the Holocaust.

After she watched the movie *Schindler's List* Linda told Barbara, "I will never forget, and I don't want anyone to forget. Someday, I'm gonna write a book." Linda didn't have the opportunity to write her book. *Beschert* intervened, and I have written it in her memory.

Linda was interviewed in 1985 by the Des Moines Holocaust Survivor Project and in 1995 by the University Of Southern California Shoah Foundation Institute. Information from both interviews was used to supplement the material I personally obtained.

ACKNOWLEDGEMENTS

My grateful thanks to each person who contributed to this project; your support and encouragement made it possible for us to tell Linda's story.

Ann Fishman Baum, Linda's daughter, was the catalyst for this book. Ann has been a source of immeasurable information and support as I pieced together Linda's history.

Anchorage, Alaska:

Craig Holmes, Carolyn Holmes, Zachary Reigle, Dr. Elizabeth Morgan, Sabina Rollins.

Los Angeles, California:

Sally Bekas. Sally was born and raised in Szydlowiec, Poland. She was captured and imprisoned in Skarzysko at the age of fourteen. Sally and Linda did not meet until after they had both immigrated to America.

Des Moines, Iowa:

Rabbi Marshall Berg, Mrs. Shirley Berg, Barbara Geller, Mark Finkelstein.

Suzan E. Hagstrom, author; *Sara's Children; The Destruction of Chmielnik*

University of Southern California Shoah Foundation:

We gratefully acknowledge the USC Shoah Foundation for allowing us to use transcripts of the following testimony: Janis R., 1995 Interview by USC Shoah Foundation Institute for Visual History and Education,

Claudia Holmes

University of Southern California, Des Moines, Iowa 10/95. For more information: http://sfi.usc.edu/

Fortunoff Video Archive for Holocaust Testimonies:

We gratefully acknowledge the Fortunoff Video Archive for allowing us to use transcripts of the following testimony: Linda F. Holocaust Testimony (HVT-668). Fortunoff Video Archive for Holocaust Testimonies, Yale University Library.

For more information: http://www.library.yale.edu/testimonies/

Linda Fishman

GROWING UP

I was born September 1, 1925, in Szydlowiec, Poland. I come from a family of seven children; I had four older sisters and two younger brothers. The boys were very wanted because in Europe, it's all about the name. Without boys, the name will not continue; it's true, because unfortunately the Ryngermacher name did not survive. All the Ryngermacher men in our family were killed in the Holocaust.

We lived in the shtetl in the center of the city. My father Yisrach had five brothers and my mother Chana had about ten siblings and they were all married, so I had lots of aunts, uncles, and cousins. We had a very big family and many friends. Everyone lived close to each other, so there was lots of visiting between families and friends. My oldest sister Riesel was married and had a young son named Velvele. I used to babysit him all the time; I remember him being about three years old. Reisel and her family lived in a small house in our back yard. Our family didn't have much money but we had plenty of food. We had a nice Jewish life.

Each of us in the family had a role. Reisel was the family baker; she would make big challahs for Shabbat. My sister Kaila was the dressmaker, and my sister Frieda would knit beautiful things. My sisters sold some of what they made to people in the community.

My father owned a butcher shop, which was our family business. We sold non-kosher meat to the Catholic population of Szydlowiec. Sometimes we would have kosher meat too, so we had many customers.[1] The population

3

was about fifteen thousand people, about two thirds Jewish and the rest Catholic.

I loved my parents very much, and I adored my father. I was his favorite of the girls. I would always help him in the butcher shop in any way I could, cleaning the shop or whatever he needed. On Friday my father would give me all the bones and leftovers to sell before the shop closed at sundown. People would come and buy the bones to make soups.[2] I got to keep the money, and I would use it to buy lots of chocolate. Sometimes I shared the chocolate with my little brothers.

Every Friday my mother would give me a sack of flour, eggs, and little pieces of fat to take to Uncle Akiva to make gribenes. Uncle Akiva was my mother's brother. He had daughters but no sons; all his daughters perished in the Holocaust. He was a nice, gentle man and he was very religious. He had a little brown beard and would sit with his arms crossed on his chest. I would give him the sack of flour and he would thank me and give me a few pennies, maybe a nickel.

After the butcher shop closed on Friday my father would go to the synagogue. When he got home, the whole family would sit around the table and share a big Sabbath dinner. On Saturday morning my father would again go to the synagogue, and my mother and I would go visit one of my many aunts. In the afternoon when my father got home from the synagogue, our family would gather for the Sabbath meal, everybody all together, and our father would tell us stories from the Biblical times.[3]

At Christmas I joined my father when he delivered meat to our customers. The rich Polish people had Christmas trees decorated with fruit like oranges, apples, or pears, and chocolate bars, not ornaments like American trees. They would often give us something from the tree, like an orange or some chocolate, and maybe a little money for delivering. I really liked making the deliveries with my father.

I liked going to school even though it was hard. We went to school until about noon, and then we would have lots of homework. When our homework was done, we did our family chores. I had the same teacher from first to sixth grade. One day a week a Jewish teacher would come into the school for religious education. I attended school for six years before the war broke out.

Claudia Holmes

ANCHORAGE, ALASKA

BESCHERT

What are the images and events that you associate with the Holocaust? My first associations are of concentration camps, the gas chambers, and Hitler. Most people have a surface awareness of the Holocaust, the events that are well known and talked about. The true reality of the Holocaust is in the devastation of the individuals, families, and entire communities that were annihilated based on the ideology of one person and one political party.

The Holocaust was a genocide machine that shattered the lives of more than ten million people. People just like you and me: mothers and fathers, brothers and sisters, individuals singled out for extermination because of their faith, political belief, or physical disability. Jewish people were the primary targets, and over six million Jews were victims of the Holocaust. Hitler used his genocide machine to kill others he deemed unworthy of living; such as political prisoners, communists, people of African or Gypsy descent, and those found to be hiding or assisting Jews.

The actual scale of the Holocaust is staggering. Researchers at the United States Holocaust Memorial Museum have catalogued 42,500 camps, ghettos, and incarceration sites that existed in German-controlled areas of Europe between 1933 and 1945.[4]

The massive network of surveillance and imprisonment was ruthless and terrifying.

Very few prisoners survived the torment of the Holocaust. Of those who did, many were unwilling or unable to talk about it. My friend Linda Fishman (birth name Liba Rachel Ryngermacher; she spelled it Luba) survived as a living witness to the Holocaust. When Linda heard of people denying the Holocaust or labeling it as a hoax, she was compelled to share her experience, no matter how painful it was to talk about. Linda considered it her responsibility to educate people about the Holocaust with the hope that in raising awareness, nothing like it would ever happen again.

Linda wanted people to see the Holocaust through her eyes, to understand and absorb its impact on an individual level. She lost her home, her childhood, and her entire family to the Holocaust. She persevered against great odds to survive, immigrate to America, and lead a successful life in Des Moines, Iowa, where she raised a family and ran a business.

How I came to meet Linda is a story in itself. I was born in the 1950s, the end of the baby boom era. Stories and pictures of the Holocaust were not in my awareness until high school and college. Perhaps it was due to me being raised in a small town in Alaska, or perhaps it took awhile for the reality of the Holocaust to seep into the mainstream of conversation. When it did, the horror of the experience was more than I could bear. My solution was avoidance. If I didn't read about it or see pictures of it, I didn't have to think about it. If I saw an article about the Holocaust, I would quickly turn the page. In college, I took a class in ancient civilizations rather than a class in American History. My personal world had its own challenges, and I decided I did not have the capacity to think about something so far removed from me.

Fast forward 20 years; my daughter Carolyn, then in fifth grade, was drawn to history with a strong interest in the Holocaust and World War II. She purchased her first book about the Holocaust from the book club at her elementary school. I admired her ability to read about the Holocaust, even while I was still reluctant to think about it.

In 2004, I accompanied my daughter on a high school trip to Washington D.C. On the schedule of events was a visit to the Holocaust Museum. I was nervous about seeing the museum, although I was ready to face what I needed to learn. We entered the museum on the first level and took the elevator to the top floor. The museum is set up so that visitors walk down through the museum on one long continuous circular path. The exhibit starts with large narrative displays and timelines that describe how Hitler and the Nazi party seized control of Germany.

As I read the displays I was struck by how deliberately and systematically small freedoms were taken away from the Jewish people. Between 1933 and 1939 the Nazis passed a myriad of laws that eroded the foundation of Jewish life and created economic hardship and personal chaos. Jews were banned from owning land. Jewish-owned businesses were boycotted. Books written by Jewish authors were destroyed. Jews were prohibited from teaching, or working in fields of medicine, accounting, or the law. Jewish children were not allowed to attend school. Life became a daily struggle to survive in an increasingly hostile environment.

As I walked through the museum I absorbed the experience; the impact and the inhumanity of what happened to more than ten million people. Nothing had prepared me for what I saw and how I felt, and the visit had a profound impact on me. I was truly stunned by the ruthlessness, the cruelty, and the blind allegiance to evil by the Nazis and their supporters.

Photos, videos, and displays - the museum included an immense amount of information, all thought provoking. Even though the museum was crowded with people, it was very quiet.

One exhibit contained a replica of the typical barracks unit in the camps. The beds were nothing more than open wood slabs stacked five high, without sufficient head room between the slabs to even sit up. It was claustrophobic and demeaning; people being treated as if they were inanimate objects to be stored on a shelf. I had seen pictures of starving, hollow eyed prisoners, crowded together on the beds, barely alive. Seeing the slab beds made it real, and I silently questioned how anyone could have watched this happen to other people and not considered it an outrage.

I stopped to watch a video of the Allies burying the dead at a concentration camp after liberation. The bulldozer shoveled hundreds of emaciated bodies into a mass grave. The stiff bodies toppled over each other as they fell into the pit. Every one of those people had been somebody's child, I thought. I could not grasp what I was seeing, it was just so horrible. When the movie ended, I robotically turned and walked away.

As I neared the exit a huge wall of pictures came into view; hundreds of photos of individuals and of families; beautiful, happy pictures of parents and children, parties, and family gatherings. I was overcome with sadness at the realization that most, if not all, of those pictured had been murdered in the Holocaust. Their hopes, dreams, and memories: Gone.

Leaving the museum I was deep in thought. I thought about all the people that had been torn from their families, their homes, and the lives they had built; their hair cut off to make pillows and blankets for their captors, their personal belongings and treasures stolen and given to supporters of the Nazi party. It is inconceivable that it happened, and that our world had the capacity for such cruelty to exist then and now.

Our next stop on the tour was a visit to the new World War II Memorial. The official dedication was still a month away although it had opened for public viewing a few days earlier. Many of the students in our party searched for state-specific areas of the memorial to honor family members that had fought in World War II. Carolyn and I located the California section of the memorial in tribute to her grandfather, and snapped a picture of the Alaska section before getting back on our bus. The visit to the memorial was interesting historically and architecturally, though it was uneventful. I had no premonition of the role it would play in the near future.

Two days later I left Washington, D. C., to travel back to Alaska. Of all the places we had seen in D. C., the visit to the Holocaust museum was still very much on my mind. I thought about the insidious way the Nazis gained control, and I recommitted to pay attention to local, state, and national issues. I had voted in every election since I turned 18, although my vote at the ballot box had been the extent of my voice. Going forward, I would make it a priority to express my opinion to elected officials on issues I felt were important. I thought about how Hitler had arbitrarily sentenced people to die because of physical disability. My father had a congenital

I Survived Hitler

disability of his right leg. He was drafted in World War II but unable to serve because of the disability. If he had lived in Germany he would have been executed, and I would not have been born.

A month later I was once again on my way back home to Alaska, this time returning from a business trip to Des Moines, Iowa. I arrived at the Des Moines airport earlier than I had hoped, misjudging how long it would take in traffic. I was not looking forward to waiting at the small airport. I bought a newspaper at the lone gift store and decided to walk up and down the concourse before the long flight home. On my trek I spotted another flight to Minneapolis, already in final boarding. With high hopes of leaving Des Moines sooner, I asked to change flights; my luggage couldn't be switched on time and my hopes for a quick exit were dashed. Disappointed, but with no other options, I continued my walk up and down the airport concourse. Finally, the time came to board my scheduled flight.

Moments after I settled into my assigned seat, a man approached me and asked to switch seats so he and his girlfriend could sit together. I agreed, as it was a short flight and I was just happy to be on the plane. Shortly after take off I opened up my newspaper and started to read. The front page story was about the grand opening of the World War II Memorial that had been held on May 29, the prior weekend. I studied the pictures, remembering my recent visit to the memorial.

The lady seated across the aisle leaned over toward me and asked casually, "Could I borrow the paper when you are done reading it?" She had noticed the pictures of the World War II Memorial in the paper.

I looked over at her; she had short, dark brown hair and rounded shoulders. Even the small airline seat seemed too big for her thin frame.

She paused for a moment before adding, "I lived through World War II."

Mildly curious after my recent visit to the museums and monuments in Washington D.C, I asked her where she had been during the war. I expected her to name a city.

"In the camps," she answered.

Skarzysko-Kamienna, Poland

Czenstochowa, Poland

Bergen-Belsen, Germany

Burgau, Germany

Turkheim, Germany

Allach, Germany

Feldafing, Germany

I looked at her, stunned at the coincidence of events that had put me in the seat across from her. Just a few short weeks before, I had been given a glimpse into the horror and cruelty of the concentration camps during my visit to the Holocaust museum. Here was a woman who had lived it.

"I was just at the Holocaust Museum in Washington, D.C," I told her. "I am so sorry you had to live through that experience."

She looked at me and shrugged her shoulders.

"There is no reason for you to be sorry. You weren't even alive," she said matter-of-factly. Her voice was rich and full, and she had a strong accent I could not yet identify.

"True" I replied, "although I am still very sorry it happened to you."

I wanted to know more about her, but I didn't want to intrude on her privacy. I ventured by adding, "If you are willing to tell me, I would love to hear your story."

She studied me intently for a moment, not displaying any outward emotion.

"Okay," she said. "I will tell you."

During the short flight from Des Moines to Minneapolis she talked and I listened as I leaned across the aisle. I had to focus intently to hear and understand her over the noise of the plane. I was not aware of anyone or anything else other than the two of us. The time passed too quickly.

I told her about my daughter and her interest in World War II and the Holocaust. I knew that Carolyn would love to talk to her, and asked if that would be okay.

"Sure" she said. "I'll give you my daughter's address, she's my secretary. You can contact me any time."

She wrote down her name, mailing address, phone number, and her daughter Ann's email address. We exchanged information. When the plane landed I felt sadness that our visit was over. I wished we had more time.

We left the plane together and walked up the jetway into the terminal. She walked slowly and with a limp, the result of a recent fall. Linda didn't know where her next gate was, and I stayed with her while she asked the gate agent for directions.

I Survived Hitler

Her flight was departing from a gate quite a distance away, so I flagged down a transport that was passing by. Linda sat down on the transport. Right before it pulled away, she reached out to hug me. I was very touched by the gesture of friendship. As I hugged her back, I felt that a special connection had been formed between us that day. I realized that I had been destined to meet her. If I hadn't faced my own personal reluctance to hear about the Holocaust, I would never have gone to the museum in Washington, D.C. If I had been successful in getting on the earlier plane out of Des Moines, we would not have met. If I had not agreed to switch seats, or had not been reading the newspaper with the pictures of the World War II Memorial, we may never have struck up a conversation. *Beschert* is a Yiddish word that means "fate" or "destiny." Meeting Linda was *beschert*.

OUR FRIENDSHIP GROWS

After I arrived home I told Carolyn about Linda. She was intrigued both by the coincidence of meeting her and the opportunity to learn more about the Holocaust from someone who survived it.

I wanted to stay in touch with Linda. I bought a card to send, but it sat on the counter while I tried to figure out what to write. I wanted to ask questions, to learn more, and to get to know her better. I was still absorbing everything that had happened in the past two months; the trip to D.C. and the flight from Des Moines. I was unsure how to proceed.

Beshert intervened again a few days later, when Linda's daughter, Ann, emailed me on behalf of her mom.

Ann wrote, "My mom met you on a plane and she wants to keep in touch. You must be a special person because she's never asked me to do anything like this before."

I suspected that Ann thought it was all very odd, but had followed through on her mom's request to contact me. I was excited that Linda wanted to stay connected with me as much as I had with her. Ann and I emailed back and forth several times and found we had a lot in common, including that we both had daughters named Carolyn.

Linda did not use email so to be in contact with her, I would have to write. I sent her a small box of chocolates along with the card, and wrote that I was looking forward to the day we may meet again.

Linda quickly replied to my note, telling me she was going to save the candy till she went to Ohio so she could share it with her kids. She wrote, "Oh, how I wish I could see you sometime in my life." I wrote to her again, and asked her questions about her Holocaust experiences. She replied, "As of us meeting, it happens once in a life time. I wonder how a 13 year old girl from a small town in Poland would end up in Des Moines, IA, going through hell…but G_d wanted it this way, I thank G_d for my family and that I got to tell my horrible story hoping that something like this would never happen again."

In October Linda went to Cincinnati to visit Ann, and she asked Ann to arrange a call with me while she was there. We made the arrangements via email, and I called Ann's house at the designated time. Linda answered the phone on the first ring. *"Hallo??"* she said excitedly. Hearing her voice filled me with happiness; it was the first time we'd talked since we'd met on the plane.

Linda enthusiastically filled me in on what was happening in her life with commentary on her children, her daily trips to the swimming pool, news of the neighbors she liked, and the one she did not like. Her stories were animated and entertaining. Just as quickly as she'd answered the phone, she changed the direction of the call. "Here, talk to my daughter," she said, and handed the phone over to Ann. I was surprised at the speed of the switch, though I would learn that was Linda's way with phone calls. I also realized it was important to Linda that Ann and I talk voice to voice, perhaps to alleviate any lingering concerns Ann had about me.

"Hello?" she said, taking the phone from her mother. Ann's voice reflected a hint of both curiosity and skepticism. Unlike her mother she had no trace of an accent, as she had grown up in America. We talked easily, sharing information about our families and jobs. Any perceived skepticism melted away as we talked.

I asked about her perspective growing up as the child of Holocaust survivors. Her response was quick and concise.

I Survived Hitler

"For one thing, I didn't have any aunts or uncles. They were all murdered. They weren't given the chance to live." No extended family, no shared history, nothing.

She also remembered her mom's intense reactions to otherwise normal things.

"One day I walked downstairs to say goodbye to my Mom before I went to school. I had on a pair of striped pants. My mom totally freaked out about the stripes. She screamed at me to go change, she'd seen too many stripes in her life." She was referring to the striped clothing prisoners wore in the concentration camps.

As we ended the call, we promised to stay in touch. I knew I had a lot more to learn from both Ann and Linda.

I called Linda every few weeks. She would answer the phone with a lively *"Hallo??"* which always seemed as much a question as it was a statement.

"Hi, Linda" I'd say, "it's Claudia from Alaska!"

Linda would pause for a moment, then say *"OhmyGod,"* as if it were all one word. Then she would say, *"Calahdia from Ahlahska!"* She drew out the middle syllables of words when she spoke, making them sound rich and substantial. Her enthusiastic and warm greeting always made me smile. She would end our calls by saying "I love you from a distance!"

19

VISITING LINDA

In August, 2006, two years after Linda and I met, Carolyn and I agreed it was time to visit her. We knew it would be a valuable opportunity for Carolyn both personally and professionally. Her major in college was elementary education with a minor in history. As a future teacher, she would be able to add depth and reality to any class discussions on World War II and the Holocaust. On a personal level, I knew Carolyn would embrace the chance to meet Linda and learn about the Holocaust from a survivor.

I struggled with the practicality of the decision. A trip from Alaska to Iowa is a seven hour flight; it was surreal to be planning such a long trip to visit someone I had only met once and talked to the phone perhaps a dozen times. I knew it was a risk, though with the strong connection I felt with Linda the decision seemed right.

I emailed Ann to ask if her mom would be willing for us to visit. Ann quickly responded that Linda would love it. Intrigued, Ann decided to drive to Des Moines the weekend we were there, so she could meet us too. With our plan in place, I made the final arrangements for the trip.

On Saturday afternoon, we gathered around the small table in Linda's kitchen. We were ready to begin the serious component of our trip, hearing Linda's story first hand. Linda readily agreed that Carolyn could videotape the interview, and Carolyn had purchased a new digital recorder in preparation for the trip. Linda knew that Carolyn was going to be an elementary school teacher, and viewed the interview as an opportunity to educate more young people about the Holocaust. Linda was prepared to tell Carolyn everything she wanted or needed to know.

A somber mood settled over the room as Carolyn set up the recorder. It was eerily quiet, and I suddenly felt cold. I mentally braced myself for what I was going to hear.

Linda Fishman

GERMAN OCCUPATION

In 1938 we started hearing about bad things happening in Germany. The Germans were breaking the windows of all the Jewish businesses and they were taking over Jewish businesses. My parents told us that the Germans were making life miserable for the Jewish people, and that they didn't think it would be the end of the trouble.

Germany passed a law that stripped Polish-born Jews of their German citizenship, and then expelled them from the country. The German Jews weren't Polish citizens either. After being kicked out of Germany, they had nowhere to go and no income to support themselves.

The Jewish people from Germany started arriving in Szydlowiec. They would knock on the doors of homes and the door of the synagogue, looking for food. Beggars were a common sight at our house because everyone knew we had a butcher shop and had food.[5] Our family shared what food we could, although with a large family there were already many to feed.

We heard the stories of what was happening in Germany, but we all thought we would be safe. We lived in a small community far away from everything, why would they bother us in our small town? We had lots of very righteous people, Rabbis with long beards who studied and prayed all the time. They said nothing is going to come to our town, we are always praying to God.

In 1939 the Germans came to Szydlowiec. We knew that it wasn't going to be good for the Jewish people, based on what had happened in

Germany. I can still see the Germans coming in on their motorcycles and wearing those helmets. The Germans started randomly shooting people on the street and anyone who was running away.

We closed the shutters on our windows; we thought that would help us.[6] We thought if we didn't bother anybody and stayed out of trouble, we would be okay. We didn't have any idea how bad it was going to get.

The Germans told the Polish police what to do, and they told us what to do. And we did it; otherwise they would come in and take away everything from your house.

Before long the Germans ordered a six o'clock curfew for all Jewish people. The shtetl was in the center of the town and was surrounded by the Polish community, so it was like a homemade ghetto. It was not walled off like ghettos in other cities, but the six o'clock curfew was strictly enforced. I remember one guy, his name was Nathan. He went out after six and the Germans killed him. I remember seeing his body lying in his house.

The Germans issued orders by radio. Only the rich had their own radios, so most of the residents would go to the State House (court house) and listen to the orders on a radio at the main square. The Germans ordered us to do work that was designed to humiliate and demoralize the Jewish people. In the winter we had to scrape ice off entire streets with teaspoons, and we were freezing. Whatever they could think of they made us do.

Every year it got a little bit worse. Men would disappear, never to be seen or heard from again. There was always killing in the town. The Germans would take the only child of a wealthy family and demand a ransom for return. The parents would pay the ransom but by then, the child was already gone.

After a few months the Germans decreed that Jewish people could not own a business.

They took away our butcher shop and gave it to a Polish man. With our livelihood gone, we had no means of earning an income.

The man who got our butcher shop was a Catholic, and Sunday was a very religious holiday for the Catholics. He told my father that since he closed on Sunday, we could do business as long as he did not see or hear anything. We knew that selling on the black market was a crime, but we needed money to buy food. My father slaughtered in the back yard and we sold meat to some of the people who had been our customers before the butcher shop was taken away.[7] While my father conducted business on Sunday, we children would act as lookouts for the police. The arrangement continued for awhile; either no one told on us, or the Polish police looked the other way.

One Sunday that all changed. We children were on the lookout, and my father was working. We saw the police and an SS man, we called him Mengele, running towards our house. Mengele had been assigned to our shtetl and he was just the meanest person on earth.

We shouted to our father, "Run Dad! Run away, run away! Mengele is here!!" My Dad ran. I was alone when Mengele came into the back yard. He was furious that he had missed my father and he started to destroy everything in sight. Being young and stupid, I stopped to pick up a quarter of beef on my back and then started to run away. Mengele yelled "STOP you STUPID!" and he pointed his gun at me. Our little dog started to bark at him so he shot the dog and killed it. I ran though the back yard, zigzagging back and forth, and escaped without being shot. It was by a miracle that I got away. I ran to a neighbors' house and hid, scared and shaking,[8] until someone came and told me that my father had escaped.[9]

My father hid at the homes of relatives for several months. The rest of us stayed in our house, but it was too dangerous to work at the butcher shop again. We sold whatever possessions we could to have something to eat. Life was very bad, very hard.[10]

Carolyn Holmes

ANCHORAGE, ALASKA

As I was growing up, I was drawn to the history of the Holocaust. Being introduced to it briefly at school wasn't enough for me, I wanted to understand the why of the Holocaust and learn how such a devastating event could be allowed to happen. I read many books set in the time of World War II, books composed of fictitious stories and nonfiction texts. When a documentary was on television I watched it comparing what I had started to learn with what the photos and videos showed. The mass murder of millions of people simply because of their religion was incomprehensible to me since I grew up in a family where religion wasn't a person's defining feature, nor was it a reason to start hating someone. I wanted to understand how a normal person could turn into a Nazi who was capable of killing innocent people.

When I was given the opportunity to meet a Holocaust survivor I was anxious but intrigued. I was worried that I wasn't a person who was deserving of knowing someone's personal and devastating life story. I was just a curious individual who wanted to better understand what happened. I felt that even before I met Linda face-to-face that she expected me to share her story with others. She knew I was studying to be a teacher and that I would have a place to share what she told me. I felt privileged to hear her story and to have to chance to connect my learning with her first-hand experiences.

Linda Fishman

MY PARENTS' CAPTURE

In late 1940 all the Jews had to register. It had been six months since my father had escaped by running out of the back yard. Before my father went to register we asked our family and friends if they saw Mengele when they registered. No one had seen him for a long time, and they didn't think Mengele would even remember my father. He was only about 5'5" and he didn't bother anybody. He was a good man who tried to provide for his family.

My father thought it was safe to go register, but Mengele was waiting for him. As soon as my father entered the office Mengele jumped out from under the desk and said "I got you!" He hit my father over the head and the blood started to gush. They threw a white sheet over his head and took my father to jail. The Germans could have killed him then, maybe he would have been better off because life wasn't worth living anymore.

The little jail was in the city center, not far from our house. I ran down to see my father. When I got to the jail, my father was standing, looking out through the bars on the window. His head was still gushing blood.

I said, "Oohhhh, Daddy, what did they do to you?"

He said, "He hit me so hard, it's terrible. If you kids don't take me out from here today, you will never see me again."

We had no way to get him out. We made a plan to hire a lawyer, but by the next day my father was gone. The Germans had taken him to another jail in Radom, a few kilometers away.

A few weeks later we got news that there would be a court hearing in Radom, and we should take a lawyer. By then we didn't have anything left in the house, though somehow my mother found a good Polish lawyer. He advised her to tell the court that she and my father were separated, that she hadn't seen him in a long time, and that she had been the one who slaughtered on the black market to have food for her children. The lawyer thought the authorities might be more lenient on a woman.

I remember my mother going off in a horse and buggy to Radom. Our family was well known and well liked in the community. Many people came to send her off and to wish her luck as she was leaving. We kids ran alongside the buggy with her as long as we could, about a mile, before we had to stop and go back home.

The hearing in Radom did not go well. My parents were both found guilty of selling on the black market. My father was sent to jail for four years and my mother was sent to jail for two years. I never saw or heard from my mother or father again.

With our parents gone and the butcher shop gone, we sold whatever we had left to buy food. The Germans knew we had five girls in the family and no parents at home. Sometimes they would come by and try to bother the girls, or they would just take whatever they wanted from our house. We had a beautiful couch, like a psychiatry couch, and they came in and took it. We couldn't do anything to stop them.

DRAWING WAS GIVEN TO LINDA BY A FRIEND; ARTIST UNKNOWN

SKARZYSKO

In 1942 the Germans came up with a new rule that one person from each family had to go to work for two hours. After two hours, you could go home. They wanted young people ages fourteen through eighteen.

I was the bravest of the sisters, and volunteered to go. I told my sisters, "You stay and take care of the little boys; I will go to work for two hours." I figured it was no big deal. I reported to the square by the courthouse. When I got there, lots of young people were already waiting.

The Germans said someone from our family could bring us some clothes. I thought, we are going to go work for two hours, why do we need clothes? My sister went home and brought me a bundle of clothes. Suddenly we were surrounded by SS men pointing rifles at us. We looked at each other and said, "What's going on here? We volunteered to go work for two hours!" And that's how they got us. After that they wouldn't let anyone talk to us or get near us.

Next thing we knew, we were being loaded standing room only onto the back of open trucks. They drove us ten kilometers to a fenced camp outside Skarzysko. The Germans ordered us off the trucks. We just stood there looking around at the fences, wondering what was happening. My cousin Friedman was part of the group. He was a good looking guy, about seventeen years old. He was furious that he had been tricked and he tried to escape. The Germans shot him dead right in front of us.

We were taken to barracks inside the fenced compound. There were three barracks, A, B, and C. The girls and boys were housed in separate barracks. I was put in Barracks A with about a hundred other girls.

The barracks had bunk beds stacked five high. The beds were like wide wooden shelves. They were built so close to each other that we had to stoop down to get in so we wouldn't hit our head. Ten girls slept in each bunk. We slept on the bare wood with hardly any straw. If someone did have straw we would try to steal it from each other.

The Germans took over the Polish ammunition factory. It was huge, and it covered almost a whole city block. The company that ran the factory rented prisoners from the Germans as slave labor. We were the prisoners. Some Polish people worked at the ammunition factory too, but they earned money and could go home at night. We had no idea how long we were going to be there or how bad it was going to get. There was no way to escape and no one to complain to; we always had rifles pointed at us.

Every day started out the same way, with a bugle call and an announcement over the loudspeaker: "Up! Up! Up! It's time to go to work!"

We would get up at six o'clock, get dressed, and leave for work at 7 a.m. We wore regular clothes. The guards would open up the gates and we would go to work. On the way to work at the ammunition factory we walked by a tree where three dead men were hanging. The Germans left them on the tree for a long time for us to see. It was a reminder that if we didn't do every little thing, we could be next.

Every day was a black day, it was just so bad. We worked twelve hours a day. The work was very hard and the Germans were vicious. We had very little to eat; a piece of bread and a bowl of soup with maybe some noodles in it for lunch, and a piece of bread at night.

A Polish man who had been a customer of our butcher shop also worked at the factory.

Sometimes he would bring me a piece of bread with a note from my sisters. They would fill me in on what was happening in town.

The nights were terrible. We were so exhausted. You lay down on the bed, finally, and the straw, when we had straw, was good. You fall asleep and then the bed bugs start to bite. So you wake up startled from the bites, can't sleep, and the bugs just keep biting. It was horrible.

We had selections almost every night. A selection is who will live and who will die. The guards would come into the barracks at three or four o'clock in the morning and yell "UP! OUT!" They would chase us out of the building and rush us into small groups outside to be counted.

The guard would walk by the groups and point at people..."You, you, and you..." If you were selected, that means you are going to be taken out and killed. People who were sick or weak were more likely to be called out, but it didn't always matter. Lots of people could still work but the Germans just decided they wanted to kill you. My friends, so many of my good friends, were taken away in selections never to be heard from again.

My first job at Skarzysko was to pick up buckets of bullets and dump them in a big container. I stood all day in some kind of soapy water and when I picked up the buckets, the water would run out of the bottom. The work was backbreaking and the buckets were very heavy, but I worked as hard as I could.

My first cousin Luba Raisel worked near me in the factory. She was three years older, she was beautiful and very nice, and she also worked very hard. One of the guards was obsessed with her, and he hated her with a passion. He was Polish, but he said he was a German. He was so mean. Neither of us could figure out why he hated her. He would come up and kick her hard for no reason at all, and then tell her, "I have to kill you, I have to kill you." She lived in constant fear for her life.

Two weeks after I arrived at camp I got very sick. I could hardly move. Typhus had been an epidemic in Szydlowiec. It was very contagious. My little brother had typhus, and I had carried him home from the hospital by piggyback. I got typhus from him.

I was afraid to tell the guard that I was sick. I thought for sure he would kill me because he wanted to kill my cousin for no reason. I walked up to him and said, "Your Honor, if you want to kill me, you can kill me. I cannot work anymore, I am sick."

Instead of killing me right then, he called in a Polish Red Cross nurse to see if I was making it up. He wanted to kill my cousin, but he called a nurse for me? It was amazing. The nurse came over, touched my forehead, and screamed, "Typhus! Typhus! Out! Out!!" as she waved frantically toward the door.

I went outside and sat on a bench. Every nick of my body hurt. I curled up in a ball and rocked back and forth. I didn't have even a sip of water though I was burning up with fever. Soon a horse and buggy came to take me to the hospital in Skarzysko. The old man driving the buggy told me to get on. I sat at the end of the wagon with my feet dangling over the edge. Next to me was a dead man in an open casket. The road was uneven and bumpy and every time the wheels jolted the wagon, I moaned in pain.

The Germans had taken a house away from someone and made it into a hospital.

I was put in a very big room in the hospital.

Someone asked me in Polish, "Little girl, do you have a rich uncle here?"

I said, "Yes, I do, Uncle Aron."

My uncle Aron Aport owned a soda (seltzer) factory. My mother was the youngest in her family, and Aron was the next oldest. She and Uncle Aron had always been very close.

Someone sent for my uncle and he came to the hospital to see me. They told him that I was very sick and needed a lot of help and they could take care of me, but someone was going to have to pay. Uncle Aron knew what had happened to my family, and that my mother and father were in jail. He told them to do everything they could, and he would pay for my care.

The next thing I remember is hearing the doctor tell the nurse to shave my head.

"Neh! Neh!" I said, because I didn't want to lose my long, beautiful black braids.

I slept for two weeks, unaware of anything happening around me. They could have given me a shot and killed me, and I would have never known.

I Survived Hitler

When I woke up I saw my cousin Golda, Aron's daughter, standing beside me.

"Where am I?" I asked.

Golda said "you've been sleeping like in a coma for two weeks, and we never thought you were going to wake up."

I felt my head and all my hair was gone. I was alive but I was very weak.

I started to recuperate a bit, and my Uncle Aron came to the hospital to see me.

He said, "If the doctors want you to leave the hospital, you can come to my house and recuperate. When you are better, we will figure out what to do."

I said "I am afraid the Germans will kill my sisters if I don't go back to camp!"

I asked the nurses if I could go back. Why did I want to go back to camp so soon?

At the hospital I was safe. No one hit me or beat me. There were no selections, and I had a bed to sleep in. I couldn't eat yet, but there was food at the hospital. It didn't make any sense, but I asked to go back to camp.

Uncle Aron went home and brought me a piece of bread to save for when I was able to eat.

A horse and buggy arrived at the hospital to take me part way back to camp. A German guard met me, and we walked the last two kilometers. I was still weak from the typhus, and walking was very hard. When I stumbled and fell on my hands and knees, the guard said, "Get up or I kill you. Get up or I kill you."

"Can't you have a little mercy?" I pleaded with him. "I'm just a young kid! I am sick!"

It didn't make a difference.

"Get up or I kill you." That's all I heard.

When I got back to camp, my cousin Luba Raisel was dead. The guard had killed her.

My friends saved my clothes for me, but before I could eat my piece of bread, someone stole it in the night.

43

A day or two after I got back to camp the Germans killed everyone in the hospital at Skarzysko. If I had stayed any longer, I would have been dead.

About that same time the Polish man came to see me. He told me my sisters wouldn't be able to send any more bread. They asked him to tell me that the Germans were chasing them every night and there was nowhere to get any bread. They were sick and tired of hiding, and they just couldn't take it anymore. They had discussed it as a family and decided that rather than be taken separately, they would report together to the gathering place. Whatever would happen would happen, but they would be together.

The Germans evacuated all of Szydlowiec and sent everyone to camps. My family, Uncle Aron, and my cousin Golda, were probably all taken to Treblinka. No one survived Treblinka, it was a death camp. The wagons went in full and they came out empty. Nobody did anything to stop it. My family was gone. I had survived by going back to camp, but life was not worth living.

One morning before work the guards told us to wait outside the barracks. We were going to have a daytime selection. Usually selections only happened at night.

I remember the German guard, his name was Bartenschlager. He looked like Hitler. He had a mustache, had those breeches, and those boots, and a cane, and with the guns…they were so vicious, those Germans…but clean they were, I have to say this.

The guards ordered the men to one side and the women to the other, and then they separated us into smaller groups. I was in a group of five women. I was still weak from the typhus and looked horrible. I had on a torn up scarf. My hair was starting to grow back and it was sticking out all over from under the scarf. My friends said, "Go in the back, he's gonna kill you first!" And they pushed me to the back of the group. They covered for me.

Bartenschlager didn't select anyone from our group, but he did call out a young man in the group across from us. "You," he said, and pointed his cane. When the young man was being taken away a boy in the group, maybe seven years old, cried out hysterically, "My father, my father!" Bartenschlager looked at the boy. He said scornfully, "Oh, go to your father," gesturing for him to join his dad. As the boy ran to his father Bartenschlager pulled out his gun. Bang, Bang, Bang... he shot the whole group of men, including the little boy. Unbelievable what I have seen in my life. The men were dead and then we had to go to work, so we went to work.

We did what we were told to do. That's how it went down, day in, day out.

After I got back from the hospital I was assigned a new job working on ammunition machines. A German guard stood watch over the operation, and two Polish men stood by in case any of the machines broke. The machines were like big sewing machines; the needle went up, the needle went down, and then the bullet came out. I worked on three machines at the same time. I got plenty of cut fingers from the sharp metal. One of my fingers got so infected that my whole hand and arm was swollen up. We were afraid to let anyone know we could not work or we could be killed. We didn't have any antibiotics or medicine; we used urine to heal ourselves.

We had impossible quotas to meet. We had to watch that no schmeltz got through. If any schmeltz was found the Germans would go into the barracks at night, drag out prisoners, and give them twenty five lashes; a woman twenty five lashes, a young kid twenty five lashes, and then pour water on them. It was horrible. I got a few lashes in Skarzysko. You learned to not show emotion or the punishment would be worse.

Three of the big German bosses got typhus and died. A new boss was sent in, and I remember his name was Morchin. He was not SS and he didn't wear the German uniform; he wore a grey shirt, kind of like a doctor's coat. He was not so bad, and you could talk to him a little. I remember cutting my finger on a bullet, it was a deep cut but there was no blood. He took me to the Red Cross nurse. Oy, I'm in heaven! I thought.

Sometimes we would talk amongst each other about food. "When are we ever going to have a whole bread to cut from?" we wondered. People got skinny and women didn't have their periods, which was a blessing as there were no sanitary supplies.

The Germans made our lives miserable in so many ways. We had a shower in our camp. They watched while we showered, and they would laugh at us. Sometimes at the showers we would see people from Barracks C. They worked with some kind of iron that turned them completely yellow. They didn't live long because whatever turned them yellow also killed them.

We had to sort through clothes from people killed in Auschwitz. We searched in the pockets and linings for anything valuable hidden in the clothes, like diamonds or jewelry. When we were done the Germans would give us a few pieces of clothes. I saved my little bundle of clothes and slept on it in those bunk beds.

Two of my cousins in Skarzysko were the only children of my mother's oldest brother. One cousin was very ill and she was in the hospital at camp. Her body was very swollen and she could not eat. An old man, a German, came up to me. He told me he knew my cousin was ill. He said, "I'm gonna help her!" So, he went to my cousin and shot her. He came back and told me, "I helped her." He thought he did a good thing by killing her. Maybe yes and maybe no, but what could I say?

One day my cousin Frieda was on a truck full of people standing up. As it was driving away Frieda screamed at me, "Luba...Save me! Save me!" How could I save her? I look back, I couldn't save her. I couldn't even save myself. I never saw her again.

I remember a girl named Ruby who was in our barracks. She slipped and fell when she was climbing down from the top bunk at night to use the bathroom. She landed head first onto the cement. There was blood everywhere and she was just moaning. Her brain was all smashed up. The guards took her to the hospital in camp. I went by to see her every day after work, and she would just lay there. She died after a few days and at the time, I thought she was lucky. She was dead and it was over for her.

Reisel Ryngermacher Fuchs

Freida Ryngermacher (left) with friends

Claudia Holmes

ANCHORAGE, ALASKA

It was unsettling to hear how rapidly Linda's life changed. She went from a peaceful existence to living in a nightmare of uncertainty. Her strong, loving family was terrorized and torn apart.

As Linda spoke, I could feel how afraid they had been; trying to stay out of sight, trying to protect each other. I related to the shock and confusion when her father was captured, beaten, and taken away in the middle of the night. Linda loved and admired her father, as I did mine. It would have been devastating to watch my father treated as Linda's father had been, and be powerless to do anything. I felt Linda's anticipation as the Ringermacher children ran beside their mother's carriage when she left for Radom, hoping that she would soon bring their father home. Instead, her parents were jailed and the children never saw or heard from them again. Linda and her siblings were left with no parents to protect or guide them, in a world where everything seemed insane.

I understood Linda's decision to volunteer for work, with the belief it would be the best choice for the family, and her disbelief when it turned into imprisonment. Linda's sisters tried to support her by sending bread whenever they could. At one point they wrote in a letter to Linda that they thought she had it better than they did, because she was in a camp, and they were forced to hide every night. I wondered, if they had seen the conditions in the camp, would they have still felt she was better off than they were? No one was in a good place. In the end, no matter what choices

Linda made to protect her family, they turned themselves in. I imagined the devastation of reading a letter from her family and realizing they were saying goodbye; the awareness that she was now totally and completely alone.

Linda Fishman

CZESTOCHOWA

The Germans evacuated us from Skarzysko to another ammunition factory in Czestochowa, farther away from the Polish border. I don't know why they moved us, maybe they needed more people there, and I don't remember how we got there, it was either by truck or by train.

We did the same work in Czestochowa but the conditions were better. The people were pretty nice there. We didn't have any nightly selections. The hours were still long, but the food was better. In Skarzysko the soup was like water. In Czestochowa we got a big piece of bread and a bowl of good, thick soup. We stayed there about six months.

CATTLE TRAINS

The Russians were pushing closer to Poland, and the Germans decided to move us again.

"Raus, Raus! Out! Out!" the guards yelled. "Take everything (that) you got!"

We grabbed what clothes we could and ran. The German guards herded us like cattle onto the waiting trains. They shoved us into the train, pushing more and more people into the car, even though it was already full. It was the worst experience of my whole life. We were standing one of top of the other. We couldn't sit down. The train car was horrible; it didn't have windows or a bathroom. When they couldn't shove anyone else into the cars, they shut the train up, just like they shut it for cattle. I think cattle are treated better than we were. When the train was full, it started to move. We didn't have any idea where we were going.

Every day we got one piece of bread, no soup, no other food. We travelled for about eight days, and then the train suddenly stopped.

"Why are we stopping?" we wondered.

The Germans opened the doors on the train cars. We could see that tracks had been bombed. We didn't know who had done it; maybe the Americans or the English, but the trains couldn't go any further. At the time I thought it would have been better if they had bombed the trains, instead of the tracks. We would have gotten it over with instead of dying a slow death.

The Germans took some of the prisoners to a nearby river to get a drink. The water was contaminated and half of the prisoners got sick and died. The Germans just threw their bodies off the train. Very few people were left on board because so many had died. We stayed there for eight more days without any food or water. The Gestapo beat us up because they said we stole their food. How could we steal their food on the train? Finally the track was repaired and the train started to roll again.

When the train stopped we had arrived at Buchenwald in Germany. It was the worst thing I had ever seen. I saw dead men walking; frozen, dead men. They looked like skeletons, hunched over, barely moving. They were wearing those striped prison suits. It was beyond belief. At least in Poland we did have some food.

Buchenwald did not have room for women. We waited on the train while they took off the few men that had survived. Three of the men on the train had been kapos in Skarzysko. They were good looking young Jewish men but were very mean to the other Jewish prisoners. The first thing the other prisoners did at Buchenwald was to kill those three kapos. They took revenge for how they had been treated.

BERGEN BELSEN

After the men were taken off, we continued with only women left on the train. We didn't know where we were going, and no one told us. The train finally stopped at Bergen-Belsen. I remember the sign on the front of the camp said "Arbeit Macht Frei" [11]

"Outsteighen! Rouse!!" the guards shouted as they opened the trains.

We were herded into a big, open yard area. In the distance I could see people wearing striped clothes. They were alive, but they looked like dead bodies.[12] I saw barracks, and fences all around. We stood there, clutching our small bundles of clothes so nobody would take what was inside.

A female guard with a megaphone started talking to us in Polish. She said, "You came to the best camp you ever seen! The first thing you gonna get is a shower!"

I thought, my God, we really need a shower. We've been crammed into a dumpy cattle car for three weeks.

She continued, "You gonna get a supper! You gonna get warm barracks! You just came to a haven." She talked for hours and hours and hours, while we stood there, freezing.[13]

Finally, she sent us to the showers. In the first room they told us to undress and put all of our clothes into a bundle. Then they sent us to the shower room. The showers dripped out ice cold water, drip, drip, drip. That was it!

We stood there naked, shivering under the freezing water, until we heard "Rouse! Run to the next room!"

We ran to the room, thinking it was where we would get our clothes back. Instead, the guard stood there, throwing striped prison suits at us. The bundles had a top and a pair of pants, like pajamas. It was totally random; tall girls got short pants, short girls got long pants, and so on. You took what they threw you. The short pants came to just below the knee. The girls lucky enough to get the long pj's could keep the cold out a little bit.

Then they threw us a pair of shoes, horrible, cheap wooden shoes, clop, clop, clop; not like the wooden shoes from Holland. We weren't used to wooden shoes and they didn't fit at all. We had to tie something around our feet to keep them from freezing.

We didn't get any food, not even a piece of bread.

They took us to the barracks. It was the middle of the winter and bitter cold outside. The windows in the building were broken. There were no beds, there was only a little straw on the floor to sleep on. We looked at each other and said, "Oh my God, we came here to Hell!! If we didn't come from one Hell, we came to another Hell."[14]

We lay down on the floor and cuddled together, trying to share what warmth we could. At two or three o'clock in the morning the guard came in and shouted, "Rouse! Get up! Get out! Somebody escaped!"

Who could escape, where was there to go? It was ridiculous. We were surrounded with fences with electricity. There was no escape. We rushed out into the yard and stood for a very long time, shivering in the freezing cold. Finally we were allowed to go back to the barracks.

For the next three days we got a piece of bread and a cup of coffee. It was better than nothing, but then they started to not feed us. One day all we got was a spoonful of jam. I couldn't believe it.

I asked the female guard, "Why are you giving us a spoon of jam? Can you survive on a spoon of jam?"

She told me, "You'd better shut up or else." That meant, don't talk.

She said someone went to the toilet outside, not where they were supposed to go. We all had to go stand outside. I remember a girl standing next to me, and then she died right in front of us. I thought, poor thing, thank God you are all done with this stuff.

I saw lots of kids drop dead beside me in the camps. It just became something that happened.

After the fourth day of us arriving at Bergen-Belsen we started having selections every night. During the day they tried to starve us to death. I was at Bergen-Belsen for about two months. I was getting very skinny and there was no food. I didn't know how much longer I could survive.[15]

What happened next was from God. All of a sudden I saw Morchin, my old boss from Poland, walking through the camp. He was over six feet tall and I noticed him right away. I quickly ran up to him.

"Your Honor, Your Honor, what are you doing here?" I asked in German.

"I have come to take out a thousand prisoners to work on airplanes." he said.

"Oh, please take me out from here!" I pleaded. "They don't feed us. You know what a good worker I was in Poland making ammunition for your Fatherland!"

He didn't give me any indication he would take me, and I didn't see him again, but the next thing I knew, I was out. Morchin saved my life by taking me out of Bergen-Belsen. I don't think I would have survived there until liberation.

BURGAU

We were driven by truck to a place near Burgau. At the new camp we lived and worked underground. Our job was to camouflage planes so that the Hakenkreuz could not be seen by the Allies. Lots of planes were flying around overhead; English, American, we didn't know or care which.

We worked with French people. They didn't speak German and we didn't speak French. They were prisoners too, but they could leave at night. Sometimes they would bring us a piece of bread.

The food at the camp was good. We got a nice piece of bread and thin, kind of watery bowl of soup every night. It was something to nourish the body, and compared to Bergen-Belsen it was heaven.[16]

We slept on the ground and the bedbugs were terrible. They would bite and keep us awake.[17]

My first cousin Dina, Uncle Aron's daughter, got sick with typhus. Dina didn't have the strength or appetite to eat, and she could barely swallow. I fed her tiny spoonfuls of soup, like one would feed a baby. It was a good thing we were not at Bergen-Belsen because she wouldn't have survived there. I lived through typhus and knew she wouldn't be able to eat for awhile, so I saved her six pieces of bread. She got better, but before she was able to eat the bread, someone stole it.

TURKHEIM

The camp at Burgau was too good to be true. We heard a rumor that the Allies were closing in, and the Germans evacuated us to Turkheim. When we got close to Turkheim we heard sirens, and we had to wait to get to the camp. We knew something was happening, but didn't know what. The area was being bombed by the Allies.

We stayed at Turkheim about four weeks. There was nothing to do in the camp. We had to move wood from one side of the camp to another. How many times can you do that?

The English were getting closer, but the Germans thought they could still hold their own against the Allies. The younger soldiers were sent to the front, and the older SS and Gestapo were in charge of moving us farther away from the front.

DEATH MARCH

Every piece of equipment that could be spared had been sent to the front, and there was no transportation to take us to new camps.

The Gestapo rounded us up and ordered us to start walking, and we were surrounded by SS with guns. It was mostly just kids left, seventeen to twenty year olds, because a lot of the older people had already died.

We looked so horrible that even if we tried to escape, there was no where to hide. The German people would know we were prisoners and probably kill us. The Germans hated the Jews.

We walked for days and days with no food. We had on those striped pj's and some sort of a junky blanket. At night, we would lay down in a field or by the road. The ground was wet and lots of kids got sick. In the morning whoever got up kept walking. Whoever didn't get up was left to die.

We walked through cities and towns, and lots of people saw us. We were exhausted, and we were starving. Nobody threw us even a crumb of food. Maybe it was best because we were so hungry, we would have killed for something to eat.

Finally we arrived at Dachau. The gas chambers in Dachau were already closed so the prisoner population in the camp was high. Dachau didn't have room for the women, so we waited outside the camp while the men and boys were taken in.

ALLACH

We walked another 10 km to Allach. Only one hundred fifty to two hundred of us were left, because so many had died along the way. Thousands of people were already at Allach when we got there. The barracks were filthy and disgusting, infested with lice and bugs. The lice were crawling all over us.

We got word from the underground that the war was nearing an end. They told us "the Americans are coming and to hold on as best as we could; we'd made it this far, don't give up now, try to stay alive."

LIBERATION

When I saw the Americans coming, it was the happiest day of my life. We started to run to the American soldiers, but the Germans didn't want to surrender and they started shooting.

The Americans shouted at us to "go back, go in!" and waved their arms for us to go back inside the camp. They didn't want us to get killed in the crossfire.

The Americans kept shooting and yelling at the Germans, "GIVE UP!! GIVE UP!!!"

Finally, the Germans gave up and surrendered.

People were yelling and shouting. We ran to the Americans. Some of them spoke a little German, a little Polish, or a little Yiddish. [18] They told us "Don't be afraid now, you are free."[19]

The American Army had never seen anything like us before, the starvation, the horrible conditions in the camp. They didn't know what to do with us. They tried, they gave us gum. We swallowed it because it was something to eat.

Lots of people ran away as soon as they were liberated. They left to find other family members or maybe to go back home. Most of us didn't have anywhere to go, so we stayed.

The Americans started to cook lots of food for us. After so many years of being malnourished our bodies were dried out and couldn't handle a lot of food. People ate and ate, and their stomachs got bloated. A lot of people died, mostly men. I got bloated from eating and I couldn't believe how big I got. I was lucky I didn't explode.

People were dying from malnutrition, and they were dying from eating food. We were infested with lice and bugs, and people were sick with typhus. The Americans decided to quarantine us to prevent anyone else from getting out and spreading typhus. They started with showers and cleaning us up. The Red Cross came in and started delousing everyone. It took two or three weeks for all of us to get cleaned up and disinfected.

One day I was outside in the yard, standing by the fence, and a boy walked up to the other side. He was unbelievably skinny, really a pity to look at.[20] He had very little hair because his head had been shaved.

He asked me "Do you know by chance a Dorothy Dorfsman?" Dorothy was his cousin and he was trying to find her.

I told him I did. We had been in the same camps since the beginning and had shared a bunk. She ran away when we were liberated to try to find her husband.

The boy told me his name was Ansel Fischman, and he asked me where I was from.

"Szydlowiec, Poland," I told him. He was from Warsaw, and he had been liberated at Dachau. We talked for awhile and then he left.

He came to Allach again to see me. He said, "I don't look so good now after the concentration camp, but I have a room near Dachau. If you want, I can try to get you out of here."

I told him, "Forget it! I am going to stay with the Americans because they will help me, and I don't know you." As far as I knew my family was dead, and I had nowhere to go. I needed someone to take care of me. He left to go back to Dachau.

We stayed at Allach until everyone was cleaned up and had seen a doctor, then they divided us up by age group and sent us to a DP camp.

FELDAFING

At Feldafing they grouped the young girls together, the older girls together, and the boys together. I was in a room with ten girls and we all had beds. The Red Cross gave us food and clothes. We had to learn to be human again. We could have used psychiatrists, psychologists, but that wasn't the way back then.

I met a really nice young man, his name was Phil. He was very gentle and kind and he adored me. We dated, we were kind of engaged, but we didn't have any rings. Every day the Jewish Relief organizations would come to the barracks to take people to Palestine. Phil wanted to go and every day he would ask me to go with him. I would say, "Maybe tomorrow, I don't feel like going today." And that went on for awhile. I didn't have anywhere else to go, but I wasn't ready to go to Palestine.

One day I was standing in the hallway of the barracks and I saw two men walking towards me. One of the men had beautiful, wavy blond hair and steel blue eyes.

It was Ansel! He looked so different than when I had seen him by the fence at Allach, several months earlier.

"Oh, Ansel!" I said. I was surprised and happy to see him.

He walked up to me and said, "I have been looking for you all this time, I didn't know where you went! I came to take you out from here!" [21]

I told him I had a boyfriend, and that we were going to go to Palestine. Ansel wanted me to leave with him and he was very persistent. Phil found out about Ansel, and he begged me to stay.

"Don't do it, don't marry him!" he pleaded. "We are going to Palestine!" He kissed my feet, he kissed every toe.

It was a long struggle, but I decided to go with Ansel. I wanted someone who was decisive and who would take care of me. I took my girlfriend Regina, and we all took the train to Dachau. Regina and I stayed in Ansel's room with him.

One day he said to me "I'd like to marry you." Plain and simple. I borrowed a wedding dress, and we were married on December 24, 1945.

The Rabbi couldn't come and neither could my friends, because some trouble had broken out at Feldafing and no one could leave. The Bürgermeister performed the civil ceremony, and Yisrach, Ansel's cousin, performed the Jewish ceremony. If you don't have a Rabbi, any Jewish person can perform the religious ceremony. Ansel put the ring on my finger, and I was a married woman.

We lived in Dachau for five years, and it was terrible. A lot of Germans resented that we had survived. We lived close to the concentration camp, but I could never go and see it.

We tried to get a visa to go to Palestine, then came Israel and we tried to get a visa to Israel, but we couldn't get out. Then we registered for America. We didn't have any relatives in America to sponsor us, so we had to wait for the quotas. Ansel registered to go to America as an upholsterer, because having a profession helped with being able to immigrate. He learned the trade as an apprentice in Warsaw. He started when he was twelve or thirteen, and would ride his bike into Warsaw every day to work. During the war he was forced to do upholstery for the homes of Nazis, which he had hated.

I didn't have any family left, and I desperately wanted one. I tried to have a child. I had three miscarriages, and my back was hurting all the time. In my third pregnancy, I miscarried at five months and almost bled to death. I didn't know what to do.

I went to a German doctor for help. He told me dismissively, "You can never have a child." I went to another German doctor. He was horrible. He told me in German, "When you go to Palestine, maybe you have a one pound baby."

I was brokenhearted. I talked to some other people, and they told me about a Jewish doctor that spoke only Polish. They said, go talk to him, maybe he can help.

I went to see him and told him the story. He told me my uterus was tipped too far back. It was probably from schlepping the heavy buckets and other work we had to do in the camps. He couldn't promise I would have a baby, but he could make two cuts and move my uterus forward a bit and that may help. If that didn't work, he could do a caesarian procedure where they make a long cut to your stomach. I was scared, but what could I do? I didn't have anybody and I wanted a family.

He did the procedure where he made the small cuts and moved my uterus a bit, and told me not to get pregnant for six months. I didn't last six months; I was pregnant in three months.

My husband would not let me see a doctor the entire time I was pregnant. He blamed the doctors for my miscarriages. I stayed in bed the last three months of my pregnancy.

When I started to have pains, he wouldn't let me have the baby in Dachau. We took a taxi to a hospital outside of the city. My water broke on the way to the hospital.

My daughter was born in September, 1949. She had jaundice and her eyes were yellow. The doctor was the same German that I'd see before, and he was a mean son-of-a-bitch. He told me, "See, I told you that you would have sick baby."

I named my daughter Chana Ita, after my mother and my husband's mother. In the Jewish faith it is very important that after someone dies you give them a name, to name a child after them.

My daughter had her days and nights mixed up. She slept the whole day and cried all night. All the Germans in the apartment building were mad at me. I tried everything to keep Chana awake during the day, and I even tried holding her eyes open! It didn't work. My husband would sit by the cradle at night, leaning back in his chair with his eyes closed, and rock the cradle with his foot.

IMMIGRATING TO AMERICA

HIAS helped us immigrate to America in 1950.[22] We came over on a big ship, the General Sturgis, with hundreds of other people. We stayed in a room with other families that had babies.

When we arrived in New York people asked us where we were going. We showed them the papers, and they said, "Ohhh, you are going to Dismoynis, Yova? You gonna be on a farm." They didn't know how to pronounce Des Moines, Iowa.

We came to Des Moines by train. Rabbi Weingart's wife and Mrs. Rose Biber[23] met us at the train. They both spoke Yiddish, which was good because we didn't know any English. They took us to a room on the fourth floor of the Elliott Hotel and gave us $30. We didn't have food or anything to cook with, but the room did have a little hot plate. My husband was too shy to leave the room, so I went to the Rosenburg restaurant across the street to get us something to eat.

After three days in the hotel, the Jewish Federation rented an apartment for us at East 13th and Des Moines Street. It was a terrible place. The apartment was very dirty and run down and there was no place to wash clothes. I washed diapers every day by hand and hung them out to dry, except for the Sabbath, so I washed them on Sunday instead. The owner of the apartment building wouldn't let me hang out any diapers on Sunday. He just yelled and yelled at me.

It was a very hard transition to America. Everything was new and strange. We didn't know the language, and we didn't know anyone. We were told to change our Yiddish names to American names to help us blend in better. They took us to doctors so we wouldn't have children and create a burden for anyone. I didn't want people to pity me, but some sympathy for what we had been through would have been nice. People didn't want to listen. They told us they had suffered through a Depression. They thought that was the same as being in a concentration camp. Did they have guns pointed at them all the time? Were they beaten and starved? Was every member of their family murdered?

People called us refugees, greenies, and greenhorns. They were afraid we would bring in disease. We did not feel accepted by the community for many, many years. We learned to keep to ourselves and not talk about it.

My husband went to work at Schmidt and Henry's furniture store for seventy five cents an hour.[24] It wasn't much, but it was enough to buy food. We bought a small buggy for little Chana to sit in, and I would walk to a store nearby where they spoke Yiddish. I didn't know what things cost so I would give them money, and they would give me change.

My husband worked at Schmidt and Henry's for about two weeks, and then there was a strike. We didn't know what that meant. He would have gone to work but people told my husband, don't go to work, they will beat you up, they will hit you.[25]

A man named Mr. Levine helped my husband find an upholstery job at Gables.[26]

We desperately wanted out of the apartment, and we saved our money to buy a house. Mr. Levine found a bungalow owned by the government. It was in such bad shape that no one would put a bid in on it. We put in the highest bid we could, without seeing it first. We got the house and it was a dump. The ceiling fell down. We didn't want to ask anyone for help so we fixed it up ourselves, little by little.

In 1951 I was pregnant with our second child. I had a dream that my grandfather was standing quietly beside me. It was the one and only time my grandfather appeared to me in a dream. He had a big red beard and he was a good looking guy, sort of blondish. I woke up, startled. I knew he wanted a name.

I told Ansel, "Oh, I just saw my grandfather and he was standing right beside me! If we have a boy, I want to name him after my father and my grandfather." Ansel agreed, and we gave our son the Yiddish name Moishe Yisrach. We called him Morris.

My husband was laid off from Gables in 1953, and we started a small upholstery business of our own. We rented a place on Harding Road for $10 a week, and asked other Jewish people to spread the word about our business. My husband had hands of gold, and everything he touched came out beautiful.

I thanked God that after miscarriages and hard pregnancies I had two beautiful children. Lo and behold, ten years after Morris was born, I was pregnant! When I was in labor with my third child, Uncle Akiva appeared on my right side. "Ohhhh, he wants a name!" I said. We named our son Akiva Alter, after my uncle and my little brother. We called him Steve.

That's another reason why I believe in God in Heaven. I never saw my grandpa again, and I never saw my uncle again. They only came to me one time. I think that God wanted me to survive, and my family wanted me to survive. If I had been killed in the concentration camps, nobody would have been left from my immediate family. I was the only one left who could give them a name.

In the early 1960s Germany started to pay pensions to Holocaust survivors. To qualify for a pension we had to be interviewed. I went to Chicago and talked to a man, and I didn't know he was a psychiatrist. He asked me a lot of questions, and I told him my story. He told me that I should see a psychiatrist every month, and I figured that meant I was going to get a pension. My husband thought only stupid people went to psychiatrists, but he went for an interview and got a pension too. It wasn't a lot of money, but it helped with expenses.

My husband could never forget his time in the concentration camps, and he could never talk about it. He internalized everything. He had horrible nightmares and would throw himself out of the bed at night, screaming, "They gonna kill me, they gonna kill me!"[27]

Sometimes he would hurt his head, and a couple times I got punched during the nightmares. He just had such terrible dreams.

He was in the worst camps; Belzec, Majdanek, Buchenwald, Auschwitz, Kaufering III, Sachsenhausen,[28] and Dachau. Belzec was a death camp, and very few survived.

Men were generally treated much harsher than women in the camps, but my husband's experiences were the worst I heard of from anyone.

In Auschwitz he was hung by a rope twice, and cut down just before he died. The Germans would hang people for sport. One time they cut him down so they could hang ten Jewish doctors instead. If the Germans let you survive, sometimes you had to put the rope on the next person.

He worked right next to the gas chambers in Auschwitz. His cousin saved him from a selection one time when he had blisters on his face. She dragged him away and hid him in the barracks. If she hadn't, he would have probably been killed.

My husband was quick to anger and was very hard on the children, especially the two oldest. We spent our teenage years in concentration camps. Our teenagers wanted things like bikes and cars. Their lives were so different than ours had been at the same age. He thought the kids had it too easy. He told them he'd had to work hard for everything he had, and they did too. That included education. He told the children that "education is the only thing that can't be stripped from you. Everything else can be taken away."

By 1969, life was settling down, and my husband was starting to mellow. We had lots of friends. I loved to entertain and have big dinners at our house. The upholstery business was doing well, and Steve was the only child still living at home.

My husband had a knot in his neck that didn't go away. We went to a local doctor who told my husband to his face that he had three months to live. He was diagnosed with late stage Hodgkin's Lymphoma. My husband accepted it as a death sentence, and he would not fight. Every time we passed by the cemetery he would look at the graves through the window, but he would not talk about it.

I took him to the Mayo Clinic in Rochester to see if they could do anything. The local doctor told me I would be wasting my time and wasting my money, but I went anyway. The people in Rochester were very nice, but they told me there was nothing they could do; if we had come earlier, maybe, but by then it was too late.

My husband never had any peace on this earth. The night before he died at Mercy Hospital he woke up from a nightmare screaming, "Take me out from here, they gonna kill me here!" The Nun went to him and said "Mr. Fishman, you are not in a concentration camp now, you are in a good hospital." [29]

He died the next morning.

My husband was only forty nine years old. He never got to see a kid married, never got a grandchild. He was a good man, a very smart man, but he was so tormented. I tell him, wherever you are, may God give you peace. I go to the cemetery and talk to him. Does he hear me? I don't know. No one ever comes back from the grave.

After my husband died, I was on my own with a child to raise. His pension stopped too, because Germany didn't have to pay it to surviving spouses. Money was very tight and it was hard to make ends meet.

My husband had been the one to meet with customers and give estimates, while I worked in the shop. Our upholstery business had a very good reputation, though people associated the business with my husband more than with me. I taught myself what I did not already know about running the business. I worked very hard, and I developed my own reputation. If people wanted excellent upholstery work, they came to me. I stayed in the shop at 15th and University for five more years, and then I sold the business.

I set up an area in my basement and did a little upholstery work from there for several more years.

I was very careful with money. I saved as much as I could and bought an annuity. When people would tell me I needed new things, like a new car, I'd ask, "Why do I need a new car? I have a car! If it works, I don't need to replace it!" I waited forty years to remodel my kitchen. Maybe I should have done it sooner, but it worked fine the way it was.

I am happy in Des Moines, it is a good community. I love my home. I have wonderful friends. I have three children, thank God. I am grateful to be in America.

But, why did this have to happen? I had a wonderful family in Poland. Szydlowiec was a nice community. We had a business, we had lots of family, lots of friends, and we had a good life. We were happy. We weren't bothering anybody. My sisters and brothers would have all married and had children. My kids would have had aunts, uncles, cousins, and a grandmother and a grandfather. Instead, Hitler decided to kill the Jews. My family was destroyed, and my life changed forever.

Only five cousins survived from my entire family. One cousin married and moved to France before the war, and she had two pictures of my family. People hid her, so she survived. My memories and two pictures are all that is left of my family.

Some people deny that the Holocaust was real. It is unbelievable what we endured and that anyone could question that it happened. More than ten million people were killed in the Holocaust. One and a half million babies were thrown into the ovens. Trainloads and truckloads of people were taken to their deaths. Barely anyone younger than me at the time survived.[30] Thousands of prisoners who made it to liberation died anyway, from malnutrition or disease. Those of us who survived have physical scars and emotional scars. The Holocaust was real and I lived it. I survived Hitler. Do I hate the Germans? No, I don't hate all of them, just the ones that hurt my family.

Many of the survivors will not talk about the Holocaust, even to their own children. When the survivors die out, there will be no one left to be a living witness.

I speak about the Holocaust because I want the whole wide world to know about it.

I Survived Hitler

I want to call attention to it, and I want people to remember it. I tell people, stand up for human rights! I tell the story for the sake of my children, my grandchildren, and my great grandchildren. If this happened to me and my family, what makes you think it couldn't happen to yours? Please, don't let anything like this ever happen again.[31]

When we first came to America, no one would listen. The older generation would not accept us. Looking back, I understand now that it was a different time. The younger generation is fantastic. They are interested; they listen and want to learn about the Holocaust.

Some people say it's a horrible world. I don't know, I think it is a beautiful world! It's just that the people who are in it, many of them are mean. You have to make peace with your faith, with your life. People ask how I can still go around and smile. I tell them, I smile to people and cry to God.[32]

Ann Fishman Baum

SPRINGBORO, OHIO

IMPACT OF THE HOLOCAUST;
THE DAUGHTER OF SURVIVORS

Growing up was very intense; it was "survival of the fittest." Dad was a perfectionist and didn't like to see any form of weakness in us. He focused on toughening us up so we could survive. His experience was that if you weren't strong, you wouldn't make it.

Dad was very high strung, and there was a lot of yelling and criticism. Mom was the defender, and she tried to keep the peace. One time she got a tranquilizer to give to my Dad. He wouldn't take it willingly, so the doctor told mom to put it in his coffee. Dad saw some of the powder on the cup, threw it across the room, and accused her of trying to poison him.

My brother and I would wait for eruptions. I ran faster than he did, so he took the brunt of it when we were young. I didn't realize our lives were anything other than normal, it's what I knew. We kids always felt guilty. If we complained about anything, we'd get the guilt put on us about how bad our parents had it when they were our age, and how good we had it.

I was always an observer, analyzing, what makes sense, what doesn't apply. Reading was my escape; I could go to other worlds that way, I could go anywhere.

The Holocaust was my mom's defining life experience. Reading about it is very emotional for me, the pain that was experienced; I can almost sense it, my aunts and my uncles, was it them? I can't wrap my head around how one human can harm another, maiming or killing them, and how other people could think it was okay.

I started to understand my mom better when my daughter was a teenager. From the stories she told, her parents sounded lovely, with a nice household. My mom had to grow up away from family, at such a vulnerable age. She never had the opportunity to be a teenager. She had to be grown up, taking care of us, making a living; she didn't have a chance to work through her feelings. After Dad died, she said "I will never let anyone shut me up; I will say what I want." She became more outspoken and opinionated, though she strived to be more diplomatic, citing her friend Barbara Geller as a role model.

My mom taught me to stand up for myself and to say what is on my mind, but it can be like walking a tightrope. My instinct is to keep a low profile because of my Jewish heritage, even in America.

I admired and appreciated so much about my mom; her strength of character, her ability to survive and thrive, her work ethic, her energy level. She was a fighter, and she was always for the underdog. Even with all she had been through, she maintained a good attitude with the world.

Claudia Holmes

FAREWELL

Ann and Linda were scheduled to take a trip to Poland in September, 2010. It would have been Linda's first trip back to Poland. She and Ann planned to visit Linda's hometown of Szydlowiec, as well as Dachau and Warsaw. Ann was looking forward to the trip, hoping to get some answers and have some long-overdue conversations about her mom's history.

She hoped to get an understanding of the life her mother would have had, if the Holocaust hadn't happened. Ann was a little concerned about how Linda would react when she saw her home in Szydlowiec, which is still standing. Would she make a scene with the current owner?

Ann and Linda never got the chance to make the trip. Just days before they were to leave for Poland, Linda was diagnosed with liver cancer.

Ann emailed me shortly after the diagnosis. "Mom's cancer is back," she said. "The doctors said she has three months."

Linda had successfully fought pancreatic cancer just a few months earlier, and the new cancer diagnosis was devastating.

Shocked and deeply saddened, I called Linda immediately.

Linda answered the phone, *"Hallo?"* her voice without its usual energy.

"Hi Linda, its Claudia from Alaska," I said.

"Oh," she said sadly, "I have very bad news."

"I know, Linda," I said softly. "Ann just emailed me. I am so sorry."

"It's the end of a love affair with life," Linda said pensively. "We all have our time."

We had spoken so many times on the phone over the years, and I always enjoyed our conversations. Linda had lived through so much, yet I couldn't imagine her not being here, her sense of humor, her unique perspective, and her amazing energy.

Linda said of our friendship, "the two of us, we just clicked." It was true, from the moment we met each other we connected. Linda was my friend and my teacher.

I called often in her last days to let her know I was thinking of her. Some days she would talk for a few moments, and other days she didn't have the energy to talk. Many people stopped by to see her and she was never alone. Linda wanted to stay home as long as she could before going to the Hospice for her final days.

Ann was scheduled to drive to Des Moines and spend several days with her mom. The morning Ann was leaving Cincinnati I called Linda, but there was no answer at her house. I thought that was odd, and I left her a message letting her know I was thinking of her. Ann was arriving that day, and I thought Linda was resting in anticipation of the visit.

The next morning Ann called me.

"My mom passed away yesterday morning," she said.

Linda had asked to be taken to the Hospice two days earlier, and had passed away the next morning. It had only been three short weeks since her diagnosis.

Linda overcame her initial shyness to be a living witness of the Holocaust, sharing her story with hundreds of people. Every opportunity she had she would educate people about her experiences. She was a voice for those who would not or could not talk about it. She was a voice for her husband and her family, and their memory lives on because of her courage and willingness to speak out.

In memory of Ryngermacher family of Szydlowiec, Poland:
(Birth years of Linda's sisters and brothers are approximate, from Linda's records)

Yisrach Ryngermacher (Father)	
Chana Ryngermacher (Mother)	
Reisel Ryngiermacher Fuchs	1915 - 1943
Velvele Fuchs (Reisel's son)	1940 - 1943
Kaila Ryngermacher	1917 - 1943
Resha Ryngermacher	1920 - 1943
Freida Ryngermacher	1923 - 1943
Luba Rachel Ryngermacher Fishman	1925 - 2010
Benjamin Alter Ryngermacher	1929 - 1943
Shalom Ryngermacher	1931 –1943

Linda's husband:
Anschel Fischman   May 16, 1920 – March 14, 1970

IOWA HOLOCAUST MEMORIAL, DES MOINES, IOWA
DEDICATED OCTOBER 22, 2013
INSCRIPTION

In 1942 I was forced to work in a factory and then was taken to four concentration camps. I was liberated by the American Seventh Army in May 1945. My husband, baby, and I came to Des Moines Iowa in 1950 with the help of the Hebrew Immigrant Aid Society. Life was difficult but I am happy here, where my sons were born.

Linda Fishman

EPILOGUE

PART 1: CAROLYN HOLMES

Since I met Linda I no longer feel that the Holocaust is about people in the distant past. As I continue to learn about events relating to World War II, and most specifically the Holocaust, I automatically tie the information to what I know about Linda's life. Her perspective is always on my mind. I try to place where she was, how something would have affected her, or what she must have felt as I am reading.

In college I took a genocide class which focused on the Holocaust. In our course we talked about Treblinka. I connected everything we discussed to Linda's family being sent to Treblinka. I kept thinking about the awful experiences her family must have gone through, and the sense of hopelessness they must have experienced once they realized they arrived not at a resettlement camp, but a death camp. Treblinka was a devastating place where the art of mass killings was experimented with. I couldn't help but wonder where Linda's family ended up in the camp, and what they were forced to do before they eventually died.

When I teach my students about the Holocaust I will share Linda's story. I want to help my classes understand the lives of people who lived through World War II, to help my students make a personal connection to history. The slow process of changes that were implemented, the fear of losing your family, and the hope it wouldn't affect you made people less likely to stand up against the wrongs that were happening around them. My students are nearly the same age as Linda when she took her sister's place working at the labor camp. What a connection for them to think, *that could be me and my family*. Many of my students would choose to protect their family the same way Linda stepped up to protect hers. I hope that through teaching Linda's story to my classes I can help them expand their world views, to be more aware of the world around them, and to stand up if they see something happening around them that harms others.

PART 2: CLAUDIA HOLMES

Meeting Linda had two possible outcomes; handing over my newspaper and ending the interaction, or choosing to engage in conversation with a stranger. I followed my instincts and chose the conversation, opening the door to a treasured friendship.

When Ann suggested that I write a book about her mother, I initially declined. A book was a huge risk on many levels. I didn't feel I had the knowledge or the experience to write Linda's story. I knew little about Judaism, and my knowledge of the Holocaust and World War II was limited, consisting only of what I learned from Linda, and from my previous visit to the Holocaust museum.

As a result of my friendship with Linda, I had begun to see risk differently; the greater risk being avoidance and silence. I considered Linda's compelling commitment to educate people about the Holocaust, and to keep it in the forefront of our collective consciousness. I wanted to honor what she taught me, and I wanted other people to hear Linda's story. I decided to give it my best shot and see where the journey took me.

I experienced a lot of darkness in researching and writing this book. It was hard to read about the Holocaust; the fear and confusion of the Jewish people as their very lives were being dismantled and destroyed. The Holocaust was a form of socially accepted mass murder, and I could not grasp how anyone supported it. I was sickened by how readily the

Nazi agenda was embraced, and that people turned against each other so completely.

I found inspiration and hope in brave actions of many individuals and families that risked their lives to help. We owe a debt of gratitude to each of them. Many lives were saved by those who saw through the veil of fear and propaganda.

Before I met Linda, I didn't feel my opinion was particularly important. Linda's story is a reminder that we all have an individual responsibility to speak up. When we remain silent, we allow others to speak for us. Just because a person speaks louder, or is one in a group of many, does not mean that the message is right or reflective of my values and beliefs.

While it may be uncomfortable to voice an opinion, it is a risk not to. Since meeting Linda, I have written several times to my local and national elected officials, expressing my opinion on a variety of topics. It wasn't the easiest thing to do, but I know it was the right thing to do.

I have also developed a strong interest in hearing other people's stories, especially those who have travelled on a different path than me. It has added richness and texture to my life.

I had the wonderful opportunity to travel to Los Angeles and spend a day with Linda's dear friend, Sally Bekas. She was delightful, engaging, and a true joy to be with. Sally told me stories of growing up in Szydlowiec, her experiences in the Holocaust, and of her close, forty five year friendship with Linda. I treasured our time together, and we continue to stay in touch via phone. I admit I had a "what are you thinking" moment when I booked the trip. It was reminiscent of my initial trip to visit Linda, and once again, I was very glad I took the risk. Sally is an amazing woman and I have learned much from her.

I now believe that every voice is important, and we must all be part of the conversation.

Meeting both Linda and Sally has challenged me to consider my role in the world, and to be the best person I can be.

I Survived Hitler

Manuscript Footnotes:

1 Linda F. Holocaust Testimony (HVT-668). Fortunoff Video Archive for
   Holocaust Testimonies, Yale University Library.

2 Ibid Fortunoff Video Archive

3 Ibid Fortunoff Video Archive

4 Lightblau, Eric. "The Holocaust Just got More Shocking." The New York Times,
   3 March, 2013, Sunday Review, p.3.

5 Janis R., 1995 Interview by USC Shoah Foundation Institute for Visual History and
   Education, University of Southern California, Des Moines, Iowa 10/95,
   Interview code 4914

6 Ibid USC Shoah Foundation

7 Ibid USC Shoah Foundation

8 Linda F. Holocaust Testimony (HVT-668). Fortunoff Video Archive

9 Janis R., 1995 Interview by USC Shoah Foundation Institute for Visual History and
   Education

10 Ibid USC Shoah Foundation

11 Bergen-Belsen did not have a sign above the gate; although several camps had the
   sign "Arbeit Macht Frie." Schulz, Elfriede; Bergen-Belsen Archives. (It is probable
   that Linda saw the sign at Dachau)

12 Janis R., 1995 Interview by USC Shoah Foundation Institute for Visual History and
   Education

13 Ibid USC Shoah Foundation

14 Ibid USC Shoah Foundation

15 Ibid USC Shoah Foundation

16 Ibid USC Shoah Foundation

17 Ibid USC Shoah Foundation

18 Ibid USC Shoah Foundation

19 Linda F. Holocaust Testimony (HVT-668). Fortunoff Video Archive

20 Janis R., 1995 Interview by USC Shoah Foundation Institute for Visual History and
   Education

21 Ibid USC Shoah Foundation

22 Berg, Shirley; Des Moines Jewish Federation (retired)

23 20 Janis R., 1995 Interview by USC Shoah Foundation Institute for Visual History and Education

24 Linda F. Holocaust Testimony (HVT-668). Fortunoff Video Archive

25 Ibid Fortunoff Video Archive

26 Ibid Fortunoff Video Archive

27 Janis R., 1995 Interview by USC Shoah Foundation Institute for Visual History and Education

28 Kaufering III and Sachsenhausen were identified in information obtained from Dachau Archives. Dachau Concentration Camp Memorial Site Archives; Riedel, Dirk

29 Janis R., 1995 Interview by USC Shoah Foundation Institute for Visual History and Education

30 Ibid USC Shoah Foundation V

31 Ibid USC Shoah Foundation V

32 Linda F. Holocaust Testimony (HVT-668). Fortunoff Video Archive

Linda circa 1946

WEDDING DAY, DECEMBER 24, 1945

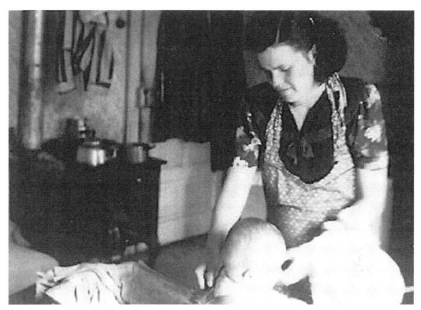

Linda and Ann (Chana), Dachau, 1949

Ansel, Ann, and Linda,

Claudia Holmes

ANSEL, LINDA, AND ANN, 1950

ANSEL AND LINDA, DES MOINES, 1968

Linda on her 80th birthday, September 2005

NOTE WRITTEN BY LINDA ON BACK OF 80TH BIRTHDAY PHOTO

LINDA TELLS HER STORY; LINDA, CAROLYN, AND CLAUDIA, DES MOINES

Carolyn, Linda, Ann, and Claudia, Des Moines

No. 143.498   143.525

Zug Tag	Lfd. №	Name	Vorname	geboren	Veränderungen
5.3.45	143 498	Goldron	Egra	2. 11. 16.	
	499	Frydman	Critta	12. 10. 20.	
	500	Frachtman	Frumi	2. 4. 26.	
	501	Rombandel	Franis	3. 10. 24.	
	502	Rynger macher	Luba	1. 9. 25.	
	503	Pogorzelec	Ida	15. 1. 27.	
	504	Lajncz Majn	Cwetla	25. 9. 20.	
	505	Bernstajn	Maria	10. 8. 20.	
	506	Tajtlbaum	Helena	11. 5. 20.	
	507	Palenker	Roza	1. 5. 20.	
	508	Garfinkiel	Rywcia	12. 12. 20.	
	509	Sullewska	Rywcia	15. 4. 22.	
	510	Zeligman	Hela	11. 3. 18.	
	511	Berliner	Pola	16. 5. 20.	
	512	Kloth	Mirjam	14. 12. 20.	
	513	Goldhor	Rachla	28. 6. 16.	
	514	Frysz	Basia	13. 9. 18.	
	515	Frysz	Felicia	15. 7. 00.	
	516	Klar	Sala	8. 5. 22.	
	517	Glikzman	Maria	2. 2. 08.	
	518	Beker	Esther	11. 9. 19.	
	519	Apfelbaum	Dora	20. 10. 19.	
	520	Feldman	Sala	2. 3. 25.	
	521	Feldman	Roza	3. 4. 20.	
	522	Goldschmid	Saba	5. 12. 22.	
	523	Jakubowicz	Pola	1. 9. 22	
	524	Jakubowicz	Sala	15. 6. 17.	
	525	Klarzala	Chana	21. 5. 23.	

HANDWRITTEN LIST OF FEMALE PRISONERS TRANSPORTED FROM BERGEN-BELSEN TO BURGAU, ARRIVAL DATE MARCH 5, 1945. LUBA (LINDA) IS LISTED AS 143,502. REPRINTED WITH PERMISSION OF SUZAN E. HAGSTROM, AUTHOR; *SARA'S CHILDREN; THE DESTRUCTION OF CHMIELNIK*

I Survived Hitler

Name	Vorname	geboren	befreit	gestorben
Rybowska	Zosia	30.11.1923 -	-	-
Rybska	Eugenia	28.02.1907 Brzesko-Nowe	15.04.1945 Bergen-Belsen	-
Rybsztajn	Cesia	20.03.1920 -	-	-
Rychel	Michalina	28.- - .1917 -	-	-
Rychlowski	Leo	04.11.1927 Derschan	-	Horgau
Rychner	Lydia Frieda	- - .- - .1927 Gleiwitz	15.04.1945 Bergen-Belsen	-
Rychnovska	Vera	01.04.1920 Praha	15.04.1945 Bergen-Belsen	-
Rychter	Paulina	-	15.04.1945 Bergen-Belsen	-
Rychter	Stanislawa	19.11.1905 -	-	-
Rychter	Tola	-	15.04.1945 Bergen-Belsen	08.05.1945 Bergen-Belsen
Rychtiger	Irka	19.08.1919 -	15.04.1945 Bergen-Belsen	-
Rychwicki	Kazimierz	14.05.1923 Lakie	-	30.05.1944 Bergen-Belsen
Ryckaert	Albert	28.06.1915 Brügge	-	26.11.1944 Bergen-Belsen
Rycyk	Feliksa	-	15.04.1945 Bergen-Belsen	-
Ryczak	Stanislaw	03.02.1914 Porabka	-	31.05.1944 Bergen-Belsen
Ryczke	Mira	17.09.1923 Zoppot	15.04.1945 Bergen-Belsen	-
Rydecka-Stepkowska	Janina	27.09.1902 -	-	-
Rydelnik	Sala	28.06.1921 Chmielnik	-	-
Rydzewska	Maria	-	15.04.1945 Bergen-Belsen	-
Rydzewski	Andre	10.04.1923 -	-	-
Rydzewski	Kazimierz	27.02.1911 -	-	-
Ryeltman	Chaja	02.02.1906 Radom	-	-
Rygal	Stefan	31.03.1904 Wiklow	-	23.04.1944 Bergen-Belsen
Rygert	Theresa	-	15.04.1945 Bergen-Belsen	06.05.1945 Bergen-Belsen
Rygiel	Stefania	-	15.04.1945 Bergen-Belsen	-
Rykala	Jan	01.12.1912 Slomkow	-	11.01.1945 Bergen-Belsen
Rylska	Wladyslawa	-	15.04.1945 Bergen-Belsen	-
Rylska	Wladyslawa	-	15.04.1945 Bergen-Belsen	-
Rymarek	Jan	-	15.04.1945 Bergen-Belsen	-
Rymsza	Maria	08.09.1927 -	-	-
Ryndak	Zdzislaw	02.05.1919 Swiectany	15.04.1945 Bergen-Belsen	-
Ryndzienicz	Wasil	08.03.1914 -	-	-
Ryng	Antonin	24.02.1927 Velharta	13.04.1945 Farsleben	-
Ryngermacher	Luba	01.09.1925 Szydlowiec	-	-
Rymlak	Stanislaw	02.12.1898 -	-	-
Rynecka	Stanislawa	28.04.1928 Jazow	15.04.1945 Bergen-Belsen	-
Ryosek	Josef	08.03.1901 -	-	-
Rys	Adalbert	09.09.1899 Nowe Miasto	-	-
Rys	Wladyslawa	-	15.04.1945 Bergen-Belsen	-
Ryschak	Leonid	08.11.1913 -	-	-
Ryschko	Petro	17.05.1902 -	-	-
Rysie	-	-	15.04.1945 Bergen-Belsen	- - .- - .1945 Bergen-Belsen
Ryster-Wermuth	Berta	21.04.1909 Dresden	-	16.01.1945 Bergen-Belsen
Ryszfeld	Sara	19.04.1922 Warschau	-	-
Ryszkowski	Jerzy	15.06.1926 Prusskow	-	16.11.1944 Bergen-Belsen

SOURCE: *BOOK OF REMEMBRANCE: PRISONERS IN THE BERGEN-BELSEN CONCENTRATION CAMP*, BERGEN-BELSEN MEMORIAL, APRIL 2005, PAGE 891. PRISONERS ARE LISTED BY NAME, BIRTHDATE, DATE AND PLACE OF LIBERATION, OR DATE AND PLACE OF DEATH. LINDA'S LIBERATION FROM ALLACH WILL BE INCLUDED IN A FUTURE REVISION OF THE *BOOK OF REMEMBRANCE*.

TIMELINE OF EVENTS

HISTORICAL TIMELINE	LINDA'S TIMELINE
	Born 9/1/1925 in Szydlowiec, Poland, a small town south of Warsaw. Szydlowiec is about equal distance from the borders of Czechoslovakia (now the Czech Republic) and the Ukraine.
1/23/1933: Hitler appointed Chancellor of Germany[1]	
7/14/1933: Nazis pass law to strip Jewish immigrants from Poland of their of German citizenship[1]	
8/1934: German president dies, Hitler and Nazi party vote to combine President and Chancellor positions and Hitler seizes absolute power[1]	
10/28/1938: Nazis arrest 17,000 Polish-born Jews living in Germany and expel them back to Poland. Poland refuses them entry. They live in limbo for several months near the Polish border.[1]	
11/1938: Nazis launch a massive and coordinated attack against Jewish businesses and synagogues within Nazi controlled areas. Windows of businesses are broken out, synagogues are burned down, and hundreds of Jewish people are beaten, taken to concentration camps, or killed.[1]	
9/1/1939: Nazis invade Poland, beginning of SS activity in Poland.[1]	Linda's 14th birthday
9/4/1939: German planes bomb Szydlowiec[2]	
9/9/1939: German Army enters Szydlowiec[2]	

115

Claudia Holmes

HISTORICAL TIMELINE	LINDA'S TIMELINE
9/17/1939: Soviet troops invade eastern Poland[1]	
9/21/1939: Orders issued to gather Polish Jews into ghettos by railroads, and to establish Jewish administrative counsels within ghettos to implement Nazi policies and directives.[1]	
9/29/1939: Nazis and Soviets divide Poland. Two million Jews reside in Nazi controlled areas, 1.3 million reside in Soviet controlled areas.[2]	
10/26/1939: Forced labor decrees issued for Polish Jews ages 14 – 60[1]	
2/12/1940: First deportation of German Jews into occupied Poland[1]	
3/1940: Germans order a ghetto in Szydlowiec. The shtetl is in the center of the city so the Germans make it into a ghetto by establishing a mandatory curfew.[2]	1940 Butcher shop is taken away from family. Late 1940 All Jews have to register.
	1941 Hearing for Father in Radom. Mother and Father are put in jail.
7/23/1942: Treblinka extermination camp opens[1]	
	9/1/1942: Linda's 17th birthday
9/9/1942: Fifty Jews sent from Szydlowiec to Skarzysko[2]	Linda is captured and taken to Skarzysko in one of the original transports
9/23/1942: Deportation of Szydlowiec residents to Treblinka. Patients at the hospital are killed. About 150 Jews stay in Szydlowiec for forced labor, though were later sent to camps[2]	Linda's sisters and brothers surrender. They are most likely transported to Treblinka, killed in the gas chambers, and buried in a mass grave.

I Survived Hitler

HISTORICAL TIMELINE	LINDA'S TIMELINE
9/30/1942: More of the remaining sent to Skarzysko[2]	
10/2/1942: Final transport; all remaining Jewish residents are sent to Skarzysko[2]	
12/1942: New ghetto is established in Szydlowiec from outlying areas[2]	
1/8/1943: residents relocated in 1942, sent to either Skarzysko or Treblinka[2]	
	In Skarzysko: approx one year and nine months
	Czestochowa: six months (est 6/1944 –12/1944[11])
	Bergen-Belsen[14]: two months (est 1/1945 –2/1945)
3/5/1945: Transport of prisoners from Bergen Belsen[11] arrives at Burgau (sub-camp of Dachau) after two weeks of travel via cattle truck. The prisoners are described upon arrival as "closer to death than life" and " half-frozen, emaciated, and starving." [13]	Burgau: one month (est 3/5-3/24/1945)[11,12]
	Turkheim: two weeks (est till mid April, 1945)
	Death march from Turkheim to Dachau and Allach
4/29/1945: U.S. 7th Army, Rainbow Division, liberates Dachau Concentration Camp[3]	
4/30/1945: U.S. 7th Army, Rainbow Division, liberates Allach Concentration camp[4]	4/30/1945: Liberated

Claudia Holmes

HISTORICAL TIMELINE	LINDA'S TIMELINE
5/1/1945: Feldafing DP camp opened[5]	5/1945: Moved to Feldafing DP camp
	12/24/1945: Marries Ansel Fishman (Yiddish name Anschel)
11/1947: Iowa Committee on the Resettlement of Displaced Persons is organized. It is charged with determining how many displaced persons Iowa can accommodate.[6]	1946-1950: Lives in Dachau, Germany, while applying for permission to immigrate
1/1948: Public discussions continue in Iowa amid concerns about resettlement of displaced persons.[7]	
4/1948: The Iowa resettlement committee urges people to write to Congress to consider taking more refugees, who upon relocation would be grateful and loyal American citizens[8]	
	1950: Receives permission to immigrate to the US (Iowa). Arrived in Des Moines 7/15/1950.
	11/15/1985: Linda is interviewed for the Des Moines Holocaust Survivor Project[9]
	10/12/1995: Linda is interviewed for the USC Shoah Foundation Institute[10]

I Survived Hitler

Timeline Footnotes:

1 http://www.historyplace.com/worldwar2/holocaust/timeline.html

2 http://www.jewishgen.org/Yizkor/pinkas_poland/pol7_00557.html

3 http://www.rainbowvets.org/wwii

4 http://www.scrapbookpages.com/DachauScrapbook/DachauLiberation/Allach.html

5 http://en.wikipedia.org/wiki/Feldafing_displaced_persons_camp

6 http://digital.lib.uiowa.edu/cdm/singleitem/collection/wwii/id/807/rec/7

7 http://digital.lib.uiowa.edu/cdm/singleitem/collection/wwii/id/844/rec/9

8 http://digital.lib.uiowa.edu/cdm/singleitem/collection/wwii/id/883/rec/11

9 Linda F. Holocaust Testimony (HVT-668). Fortunoff Video Archive for Holocaust Testimonies, Yale University Library.

10 Janis R., 1995 Interview by USC Shoah Foundation Institute for Visual History and Education, University of Southern California, Des Moines, Iowa 10/95, Interview code 4914

11 United States Holocaust Memorial Museum Encyclopedia of Camps and Ghettos 1933-1945, Volume 1, pgs 461

12 United States Holocaust Memorial Museum Holocaust Survivors and Victims Database as researched and provided by Archives, Bergen Belsen

13 Transport List from Bergen-Belsen to Burgau obtained from Suzan E. Hagstrom, author of *Sara's Children; The Destruction of Chmielnik*

14 *Book of Remembrance*: Prisoners in the Bergen-Belsen Concentration Camp, Bergen-Belsen Memorial, April 2005, Pg 891. Linda's liberation date and location will be included in a future update to the *Book of Remembrance*.

GLOSSARY

PRONUNCIATION	DEFINITION
Akiva (Ah-KEY-vah)	Linda's uncle, her mother's youngest brother
Allach (ALL-ach)	Sub camp of Dachau, 79 km (43 miles)[7] east of Turkheim
Alter (AHL-ter)	Linda's younger brother's middle name
Ansel (ANN-sell)	Linda's husband (Yiddish spelling is Anschel) (He is listed as Anczel Fiszman in the Archives of the Dachau Concentration Camp Memorial)
Albeit Macht Frei (AHR-bite Mach Fry)	Slogan over the gate of many concentration camps, translated to "Work Makes You Free"
Bartenslager (BAR-TIN-slah-ger)	SS officer at Skarzysko Forced labor camp; prisoners called him the Angel of Death.
Belzec (BELL-jeetz)	Concentration camp in Poland
Bergen-Belsen (BEAR-gen-BEL-sen)	Concentration camp in Germany. Distance from Czestochowa to Bergen-Belsen is 813 km (505 miles)[7]
Beschert (Beh-SHEERT)	Destiny or fate
Buchenwald (BOO-kin-wahld)	Concentration camp in Germany

Bürgermeister (BERG-ee-my-ster)

City official, similar to a magistrate or mayor

Burgau (BUL-gar)

Sub camp of Dachau[5] run by Messerschmitt, located 615 km (382 miles)[7] south of Bergen-Belsen. It existed for approximately two months 2/1945 – 3/1945

Challah (HAH-lah)

Traditional Jewish egg bread eaten on Sabbath

Chana (HAH-nah)

Yiddish spelling of Hannah (Linda's mother)

Czestochowa (CHEN-stih-kow) also spelled Tschenstochau

Forced labor camp 152 km (94 miles)[7] west of Skarzysko, operated by HASAG

Dachau (DAH-how)

Concentration camp in Germany, with 32 sub camps[6]

DP Camp

Displaced Persons camps were established by the Allies to care for prisoners

Feldafing (FELD-a-fink)

DP camp 41 km (25 miles)[7] southwest of Allach

Forced Labor Camp

Site where prisoners toiled as slave labor for a German business. Barracks were built close to the work location.

Freida (FRY-da)

Linda's fourth oldest sister

I Survived Hitler

Gestapo (Geh-STAH-poe)	German Secret Police, a sub-group of the SS. Primarily responsible for rounding up Jewish people for either concentration camps or execution. The Gestapo operated with unlimited authority and extreme cruelty.[1]
G_d (standard pronunciation)	Yiddish spelling of God
Gribenes (GREE-ben-ess)	Fried chicken skin, a traditional Jewish food
Hakenkreuz (HAH-KEN-croitz)	Swastika, or symbol of the Nazi party
HASAG	Hugo Schneider AG (HASAG), a privately owned company, secured military contracts to supply ammunition and small arms to the Nazis. It rented prisoners from the German government and used them as forced laborers. HASAG operated several ammunition factories during the war, including Skarzysko and Czestochowa.[8]
Hebrew Immigrant Aid Society (HIAS)	Assists and provides support for the resettlement of refugees
Jewish Federation	An area with an active Jewish community may sponsor a federation to coordinate human and support services. Jewish Federations of North America is the umbrella organization for the autonomous federation offices.

123

Claudia Holmes

Kaila (KAI-la)	Linda's second oldest sister
Kapos (CAP-Os)	Name for Jewish people in concentration camps and forced labor camps who worked for the Germans in return for better treatment than other prisoners.
Kaufering (COW-fare-ing)	Concentration camp in Germany
Luba or Liba (LOO-bah)	Linda's birth name
Majdanek (mi-DAHM-mick)	Concentration camp in Poland
Mengele (MENG-geh-la)	SS Officer that captured Linda's father
Messerschmitt (MESSA-schmit)	German aircraft manufacturer, used forced labor during WWII
Quotas	Number of immigrants allowed entry to the United States per year, per country of origin.
Pension	West Germany agreed to pay compensation to victims of Nazi persecution via the Luxembourg Agreements on 9/10/1952
Radom (RAH-dom)	City in Poland 22 km (13 miles)[7] northeast of Szydlowiec, also known as "Little Warsaw"
Raus (ROUSE)	Run
Reisel (RYE-zel)	Linda's oldest sister
Resha (RAY-sha)	Linda's third oldest sister

Ryngermacher or Ryngiermacher (RING-GEE-mach-er)	Linda's family name
Sachsenhausen (SAXEN-housen)	Concentration camp in Germany
Schmeltz (sch-MELT-s)	A defective product, used in reference to defective bullets made by prisoners working ammunition machines at Skarzysko
SS or Schutzstaffel (SHOOTS-stah-fell)	Begun as Hitler's personal bodyguards, it expanded to control all of Germany's police forces. The SS was in charge of operations at the concentration and death camps.[2]
Shabbat (Scha-BAHT) or Sabbath	The Jewish day of rest, beginning at sundown on Friday and ending at sundown on Saturday
Shalom (SHOW-lem)	Linda's youngest brother's first name
Shtetl (Sch-TAY-till)	Yiddish for town or village, the center of the Jewish community in a city
Skarzysko (scar-JISK-go)	Forced labor camp 10 km (6 miles)[7] northeast of Szydlowiec run by HASAG. Between 25,000 and 30,000 prisoners were imprisoned in Skarzysko and more than 18,000 died.[3]
Szydlowiec (SCHID-LO-vee-it-ch)	The city in Poland where Linda was born and her family had lived for generations

Treblinka (treh-BLEEN-ka)	Death camp 232 km (144 miles)[7] northeast of Szydlowiec. In the fifteen months between 7/1942 and 10/1943, 850,000 people were killed at Treblinka and buried in mass graves.[4]
Turkheim (TURK-hyme)	Sub camp of Dachau, 54 km (34 miles)[7] southeast of Burgau
Typhus	Illness spread by lice
Underground	Jewish people that eluded capture, hid in the forests, and fought the Germans
Velvele (WOLF-eh-la)	Reisel's son and Linda's nephew
Yiddish (YID-ish)	Traditional language spoken by European Jews
Yisrach (I-sek or ITS-rak)	Yiddish spelling of Issac or Icek (Linda's father)

I Survived Hitler

Glossary Footnotes:

1 http://www.jewishvirtuallibrary.org/jsource/Holocaust/Gestapo.html

2 http://www.jewishvirtuallibrary.org/jsource/Holocaust/SS.html

3 http://www.yadvashem.org/odot_pdf/Microsoft%20Word%20-%206028.pdf

4 http://www.jewishvirtuallibrary.org/jsource/Holocaust/Treblinkatoc.html

5 United States Holocaust Memorial Museum Encyclopedia of Camps and Ghettos, 1933-1945

Volume 1, Part A, pg 480-481

6 http://www.jewishgen.org/forgottenCamps/General/ListeEng.html

7 Distances: https://maps.google.com

8 http://en.wikipedia.org/wiki/Hugo_Schneider_AG

9 http://www.claimscon.org/?url=history

10 http://www.ushmm.org/outreach/en/article.php?ModuleId=10007732

Photo by Lucille Stietz

Claudia Holmes earned a business degree from the University of Alaska Fairbanks before launching a career in mortgage banking. She has a passion for volunteering, education, and travel.
A lifelong Alaskan, she lives in Anchorage with her husband Craig. They have two adult children.

Made in the USA
San Bernardino, CA
04 September 2014